A CRITICAL EXAMINATION

OF THE

PESHITTA VERSION OF THE BOOK OF EZRA

A Critical Examination
OF THE
Peshitta Version of the Book of Ezra

BY

CHARLES ARTHUR HAWLEY

Wipf & Stock
PUBLISHERS
Eugene, Oregon

Wipf and Stock Publishers
199 W 8th Ave, Suite 3
Eugene, OR 97401

A Critical Examination of the Peshitta Version of the Book of Ezra
By Hawley, Charles Arthur
ISBN: 1-59752-289-9
Publication date 7/1/2005
Previously published by Columbia University Press, 1922

TO MY HONORED TEACHER
PROFESSOR JULIUS A. BEWER, PH. D., D. THEOL.
IN GRATITUDE
FOR HIS INSPIRING TEACHING, WISE
COUNSEL AND TRUE FRIENDSHIP.

NOTE

The present Study of the Peshitta text of the Book of Ezra fills a lacuna in the literature devoted to that translation of the Old Testament. Whether we agree or not with the conclusions reached by Dr. Hawley, everyone who reads the following pages must feel certain that he has gone deeply into the subject and has made use of all the material that is available.

Columbia University *Richard Gottheil.*
1922

PREFACE

This dissertation is the outcome of an investigation begun during postgraduate work in Union Theological Seminary in a Seminar conducted by Professor Julius A. Bewer. After reviewing the adverse criticisms of the scholars concerning the Peshitta Text of the Book of Ezra, and then carefully studying the Peshitta itself, I found that the value of the latter for textual criticism had been considerably underestimated and as a result almost entirely neglected. During further postgraduate study at the University of Basel, I continued my study of the Ezra text. Finally, during the summer semester of 1922 at the University of Halle-Wittenberg, I brought this work to the point where I offer my investigations to the public.

I take this opportunity gratefully to acknowledge my indebtedness to Professor Richard J. H. Gottheil, and to Dr. Frederick Vanderburgh of Columbia University; to Professors Fagnani and Henry Preserved Smith of Union Theological Seminary; and to Professors Duhm, Alt, Wernle, and the late Friedrich Schulthess of the University of Basel; and to Professors Gunkel, Brockelmann, Bauer, and Dr. Hempel of the University of Halle-Wittenberg. To Professor Bauer of Halle and to Professor Budde of Marburg I express deep appreciation for valuable assistance given me in reading the proof. I gratefully acknowledge my special indebtedness to Professor Julius A. Bewer of Union Theological Seminary under whose sympathetic direction and inspiration I have done all my work.

University of Halle-Wittenberg in August 1922.

CHARLES ARTHUR HAWLEY.

BIBLIOGRAPHY

BARNES, W. E., Peshitta Text of Chronicles (Camb. Univ. Press, 1897).
BATTEN, L. W., Ezra-Nehemiah (New York, 1913).
BERTHOLET, A., Esra und Nehemia (Tübingen, 1902).
BEWER, J. A., Der Text des Buches Ezra (Göttingen, 1922).
BLOCH, Joshua, A Critical Examination of the Text of the Syriac Version of the Song of Songs. AJSL, 1922.
BUHL, F., Canon and Text of the Old Testament (Edinburgh, 1894).
BURKITT, F. C., Article "Text and Versions", Ency. Biblica.
CORNILL, C. H., Einleitung in das Alte Testament (Tübingen, 1913). Das Buch des Propheten Ezechiel (Leipzig, 1886).
DAVIES, T. W., Ezra, Nehemiah, and Esther (New York, 1909).
DUHM, B., Die Psalmen (Tübingen, 1922).
DUVAL, R., La Littérature Syriaque (Paris, 1907).
GUTHE, The Books of Ezra and Nehemiah, (Leipzig and New York, 1901).
KLOSTERMANN, A., Geschichte des Volkes Israel (München, 1896).
MEYER, Ed., Die Entstehung des Judenthums (Halle, 1896).
NESTLE, E., Bibelübersetzungen (Syrische Übersetzungen) PRE III.
NÖLDEKE, Theodor, Die Alttestamentliche Literatur (Leipzig, 1868).
RAHLFS, Beiträge zur Textkritik der Peschitta ZATW 1889.
SIEGFRIED, D. C., Esra, Nehemia, und Esther (Göttingen, 1901).
STEUERNAGEL, C., Einleitung in das Alte Testament (Tübingen, 1912).
SWETE, Introduction to the Old Testament in Greek (Cambridge, 1914).
TORREY, C., Ezra Studies (Chicago, 1910).
WELLHAUSEN, J., Text der Bücher Samuelis (Göttingen, 1871).
WRIGHT, W., A Short History of Syriac Literature (London 1894). The Homilies of Aphraates (London, 1869).

ABBREVIATIONS

AJSL, American Journal of Semitic Languages and Literatures.
BDB, Brown, Driver, Briggs. Hebrew Dictionary.
Esd., I Esdras Swete, Old Testament in Greek.
Esd.^{A}, Alexandrian Codex of I Esdras.
Esd.^{B}, Vatican Codex of I Esdras.
Esd.^{L}, Lagarde's text of I Esdras in "Libri Veteris Testamenti Syriace". 1861.
Esd.$^{Syr.}$, Syriac of I Esdras, according to Lagarde.
G (LXX), The Greek translation, according to Swete's Edition.
   G^A, Alexandrian Codex of the Greek Ezra.
   G^B, Vatican Codex of the Greek Ezra.
   G^L, Lagarde's Edition of Ezra.
MT, Masoretic Text.
Neh., Nehemiah.
PRE, Realencyclopädie f. Prot. Theol. u. Kirche. 3. Aufl.
S, Syriac (Peshitta).
Vulg., Vulgate.
   L, Lee's Edition of the Syriac Text.
   P, Paris Polyglott.
   RV, American Revised Version (1901).
   U, Urumia Edition of Syriac Text.
   W, London Polyglott (Walton).
ZATW, Zeitschrift für alttestamentliche Wissenschaft
+, Addition to the text.

INTRODUCTION.

The Bible of the Syriac Church, like that of the Alexandrian (Greek), was the work of several translators and was made at different times. After the ninth century, Syriac Mss. of the Old Testament generally went by the name of Peshitta. The origin of the Peshitta lies in obscurity. Internal evidence points to characteristics both of Jewish and of Christian translators.

Nöldeke[1] has stated the facts in the case as follows: "Sie (Peschita) zeigt, namentlich im Pentateuch, nicht bloß in der Auffassung, sondern selbst in den Ausdrücken eine entschiedene Verwandtschaft mit den Targumen, theils mit den officiellen, theils mit den übrigen. Man hat deshalb in neuerer Zeit auch die Peschita ohne weiteres als eine jüdische Uebersetzung beanspruchen wollen, aber dagegen sprechen doch gewichtige Gründe. Manche Stellen zeigen in ihr eine entschiedene christliche Auffassung, zum Theil in Widerspruch mit allen sonstigen alten Uebersetzungen und in einer Weise, die nicht durch nachträgliche Interpolation erklärt werden kann; namentlich finden sich solche Stellen im Syrischen Psalter. Ferner ist die Peschita, soweit wir wissen, nie von Juden gebraucht — der Verfasser des Targums zu den Sprüchen unterwarf sie erst einer Umarbeitung im jüdischen Sinn —, während sie stets bei allen christlichen Parteien

---

[1] Nöldeke, *Die Alttestamentliche Literatur*, S. 262. Cf. also Buhl, *Canon and Text of the Old Testament*, p. 186.

Syriens als Kirchenübersetzung gedient hat. Auch ist der Dialect, in dem sie abgefasst ist, derselbe, welcher im syrischen Neuen Testament herrscht und der überhaupt die Schriftsprache der christlichen Syrer bildet, deren erstes Monument für uns wenigstens eben sie ist, während wir keine jüdischen Schriften in dieser Mundart kennen."

Wright[1] similarly holds that the Peshitta is "not improbably a monument of the learning and the zeal of the Christians of Edessa. Possibly Jewish converts, or even Jews, took a part in it, for some books (such as the Pentateuch and Job) are very literally rendered whereas the coincidences with the LXX (which are particularly numerous in the prophetical books) show the hand of Christian translators or revisers. That Jews should have had at any rate a consultative share in this work need not surprise us, when we remember that Syrian fathers, such as Aphraates, in the middle of the fourth century, and Jacob of Edessa, in the latter half of the seventh, had frequent recourse, like Jerome, to the scholars of the synagogue."

An example of purely Jewish translation is pointed out by Nöldeke[2]: "Eine besondere Stellung nimmt aber die syrische Uebersetzung der Chronik ein. Diese ist allerdings ein reines Targum. Sie zeigt vielfache Zusätze, Umschreibungen und rabbinische Ausdeutungen: die Aengstlichkeit bei der Vermeidung von Anthropomorphismen ist hier ganz wie in den Targumen. Den rein jüdischen Character zeigt die Stelle 1. Chron. 5 2, wo es heisst: "aus Juda wird hervorgehen der König Messias"; wer diesen Zusatz gemacht hat, für den war doch Christus noch nicht gekommen. Bei diesem wenig gelesenen Buche haben die Syrer also ein jüdisches Targum arglos übernommen."

---

[1] Wright, *Syriac Literature*, p. 3.
[2] Nöldeke, *AL*, S. 263 f.

INTRODUCTION 3

The antiquity of the Peshitta has long been recognized. Nöldeke says:[1] "Die Peschita ist wohl die älteste aller christlichen Bibelübersetzungen. Bei der starken Ausbreitung des Christentums in Syrien und Mesopotamien schon in dessen frühsten Zeiten konnte man eines allgemein verständlichen Textes des damals noch allein als kanonisch geltenden Alten Testaments nicht lange entbehren. Für den heiligen Ephraim (gestorben 373) ist die Peschita denn auch schon ein altes Werk. Für ein hohes Alter spricht auch die Reception bei allen syrischen Secten, die sich doch sonst unter einander so bitter haßten, und ferner das oben dargelegte Verhältnis zur jüdischen Tradition."

The Edessene Canon omitted Chronicles, Ezra, and Nehemiah.[2] The Nestorians further omitted Esther. Whether this indicates that the Chronicler's work was translated into Syriac at a later time than the first translations, we cannot say. Wright points out[3] "that all these books are cited by Aphraates, and that they all appear in the Codex Ambrosianus." Later the books at first omitted were received into the Canon of the Peshitta. At what time we do not know.

No interpretations in Ezra indicate the hand of a Christian. This may be due to the content of the book which gave no occasion where a Christian would be led to make a theological gloss. The entire translation indicates the work of a most careful biblical scholar. The Syriac translation of Ezra is in no case slavishly literal as is that of the Pentateuch but it is often paraphrastic. Why should it not be so? The translator wanted to bring out the meaning of the original as effectively as possible, and he felt that this could be done in a number of cases better by a paraphrase than

[1] Nöldeke, *AL*, S. 264.
[2] Duval, *Lit. Syr.* p. 32; Nestle, PRE3 III S. 170.
[3] Wright, *Syr. Lit.*, p. 5. *Homilies of Aphraates*, vol. I. pgs. 48, 358, 376.

by a very literal translation. Thus he put into language intelligible to all who might read his work, certain phrases which, if literally rendered, would, in his time, have had no meaning.[1] In 2 63 for example, the Hebrew עד עמד כהן לאורים ולתמים is rendered by S. ܟܗܢܐ܂ ܢܩܘܡ ܕܥܕܡܐ ܐܚܪ. ܘܢܒܥܐ ܫܘܐܠܐ. A comparison with the Greek translations (G & Esd., G ἕως ἀναστῇ ἱερεὺς τοῖς φοτίζουσιν καὶ τοῖς τελείοις, Esd. ἐνδεδυμένος τὴν δήλωσιν καὶ τὴν ἀλήθειαν) shows that all three paraphrased the text but that S. has given the clearest explanation of the meaning of the ancient oracular device. G. makes no sense; Esd. is better than G. but certainly inferior to S.

Not only in this case, but all the way through, a comparison of S. with G. shows that the Peshitta version of Ezra was not influenced by G. This is against the opinion of Siegfried.[2] The cases in which S. and G. agree against MT are of so unimportant a nature that the Syriac translator may never have read G.[3] It is all the more remarkable, therefore, that Siegfried's statement should have been accepted as valid for more than twenty years. Evidently nobody has ever examined into its truth.

Again, the generally accepted opinion in regard to the independent value of S. is also false. Siegfried holds that the Syriac "ist oft mehr Umschreibung als Uebersetzung." Klostermann says that the translation is of little value due to scribal errors and the "reine Willkür des Punktators."[4] Torrey in his *"Ezra Studies"* goes even so far as to say, "the

[1] Cf. 2 63, 9 4. Any reader of the English Bible who has had no scientific training is under a handicap in not understanding such phrases as "urim and tummim", which an unskilled reader of S. would not have experienced.
[2] Siegfried, *Esra, Nehemia und Esther Handkommentar* S. 9 ("ist von den LXX beeinflusst").
[3] Cf. G & S. vs. MT 4 10 12, 5 5, 7 8, 19, 25, 8 36, 9 1.
[4] Realencyclopaedie, Art. *Ezra-Nehemia*.

INTRODUCTION 5

Syriac and Arabic versions of the canonical Chron.-Ezra-Neh. have long been known to be late and wellnigh worthless—the Arabic absolutely so—and any attempt to make a critical use or 'investigation' of them is a waste of time."[1] Batten in his commentary on Ezra[2] ignores S. absolutely; and Löhr in his edition of Ezra in Kittel's "Biblia Hebraica" uses it only three times. Others[3] dismiss the Syriac Version without a mention or hold it to be of little value. In fact, until the publication of Professor Bewer's *"Der Text des Buches Ezra"*,[4] S. has been wellnigh friendless. Professor Bewer has done much to correct the erroneous ideas regarding S.

When we undertake a comparison between the Hebrew and Syriac, we are at once confronted with the lack of a critical edition of S. The Peshitta text is found only in the Codex Ambrosianus, in the Paris and Walton (London) Polyglotts, and has been reprinted three times by missionary societies. The text found in the Paris Polyglott is that edited by Gabriel Sionita from a late Ms. This, the "editio princeps", was printed in 1645, and in 1657 reproduced in the London Polyglott. The latter is a careful reprint, there being but one variant spelling (6 19). In 1823 Lee produced an edition for the British and Foreign Bible Society. This, the most accessible edition, reproduces with slight variation the text of the Paris Polyglott. In 1852 the American Missionaries at Urumia published an edition in Nestorian characters, fully punctated and in a simplified spelling.[5] Another edition, published in 1887 at Mosul, I have been

[1] Torrey, *Ezra Studies* p. 64.
[2] Batten, *Commentary on Ezra-Nehemiah* in ICC series 1913.
[3] Cf. Steuernagel, *Einleitung in das Alte Testament*, § 17.
[4] Bewer, *Der Text des Buches Ezra*, (Göttingen, 1922).
[5] The Urumia Edition has the classical and modern Syriac in parallel columns.

unable to obtain; but from all inquiries, I learn that it has no independent value. The editions are really the same, all of them being reprints of the Paris Polyglott.

A minute comparison of the Paris (P), Walton (W), and Lee (L) gives the following result:

3 11 WP ܒܝܘܒܒܐ L ܝܘܒܒܐ.

4 2 W ܕܐܣܚܪ, PL ܕܐܣܚܪ.

6 19 WL ܦܣܚ P ܦܨܚ. This is a variant spelling. One form is as correct as the other.

A similar comparison of Paris, Walton, Lee, and Urumia (U) yields this result:

3 11 U ܝܒܒܘ ܝܘܒܒܐ WP ܝܒܒܘ ܒܝܘܒܒܐ L ܝܒܒܘ ܝܘܒܒܐ. U omits ܒ reading: "they shouted a shout of joy"; it is evidently an improved edition of L.

4 2 W ܕܐܣܚܪ, ULP ܕܐܣܚܪ. The mistake is in W. Cf. above.

4 10 WLP ܐܣܢܦܪ U ܐܣܢܦܪ. Here an attempt has been made to bring U closer to MT — אסנפר.

6 9 LP ܦܣܚ WU ܦܨܚ. Variant spellings of the same word.

8 26 WPL ܒܐܝܕܝܗܘܢ U ܥܠ ܐܝܕܝܗܘܢ. Here U has been corrected by MT which reads על־ידם.

9 2 WPL ܘܥܡܡܐ U ܒܥܡܡܐ, MT בעמי.

From this comparison, it is evident that U was made with MT at hand as a corrective.

In the following particulars also U differs from PLW: a) Ribui is often omitted in the plurals; b) ܗܘܐ is omitted in 5 15; c) simplified spelling is considerably used, *e. g. yodh* and *aleph* are omitted in such words as ܐܝܣܪܐܝܠ (PLW) which U writes ܐܣܪܝܠ.

It is apparent that for all practical purpose these various editions are of equal value, since they all represent one and the same text. I have used *L.* because it is the most convenient.

Unfortunately, the Mss. of the Book of Ezra have not

been collated since the collation by Thorndyke of the Usher, Pococke, and Cambridge Mss. in vol. vi of Walton's Polyglott, which is reproduced here: 2 13 ܘܐܝܒܝܗܘܢ] nostri, ܘܐܝܒܝܗ. 2 20 ܘܣܡܐ] nostri, ܘܣܡܠܐ. 2 25 ܘܐܕܥܟܝ ܐܡܪ] nostri, ܐܠܐ ܡܝ ܐܕܥܟ ܐܡܪܘ. 2 22 ܡܥܕܪ] Uss. ܘܣܩܥܪ. 2 36 ܒܦܘܡܢ ܒܠܚܕ] nostri, ܠܒܠܚ. 2 43 ܪܒܢܠ] nostri, ܪܒܢܠܐ. 2 46 ܡܠܥܕܢ] nostri ܡܠܥܕܢܐ. 2 52 ܐܪܣ] Poc. ܐܪܣ. 2 47 ܐܡܐ ,ܐܡܐ ܢܝܗܝ ܢܝܗܝ ܢܝܗܝ] nostri, ܐܒܐ, ܒܝܒܘ ܒܢܗܝ. 2 70 ܘܡܫܥܒܕܝܢ] Hebr. postulat ܚܡܣܢܘܒܝܗܘܢ. 3 5 ܠܟܬܒܐ] nostri, ܠܟܬܒܐ scribe ex Heb. ܘܡܠܒܒ. 3 9 ܘܡܒܝܢܗܝ ܘܕܬܢܘܒ-] nostri, ܪܘܒܐ. 4 5 ܠܡܕܚܩܬܐ] lege ܠܡܕܚܩܬܐ etsi contra libros. 46 ܐܣܒܝܢܢ ܘܕܒܕܚܠܬܗ] ܘܐܒܘܢ. ܘܕܒܕܚܠܬܗܘܢ. 4 10 ܐܨܥܪ] nostri, ܘܐܨܚܪ. Ib. ܘܐܚܕܬ] nostri ܚܒܕ ܬܐܪ. 4 11 ܘܐܚܕܬ] nostri ܐܘܚܕܬ. 4 13 ܚܠܝܡ ܒܐܪܝ ܠܝ] Poc. omittit ܠܝ, item Uss. 4 17 ܢܘܡ] lege ex Heb. ܡܝ ܢܐ etsi invitis libris. 4 18 ܐܥܐܟܝܒܝ] nostri, ܐܥܐܠܠܒܝ. 6 4 ܚܕܒܘ] nostri, ܚܕܒܘ male. 66 ܐܢܣܒܘ] nostri, ܐܢܣܒܘ male. 6 13 ܕܥܟܝ] Uss. ܘܐܠܒܝ: Potius deesse puto ܒܠܚܡܐ e chald. 7 15 ܒܠܚܡܐ] Poc. ܒܠܚܡܝ. Uss. ܒܠܚܡܝܗܘܢ. 7 17 ܐܠܐ] nostri ܐܠܘ. 8 1 ܐܡܬܩܒܐ] Hebr. ܐܡܬܩܒܝܘ libris non obstantibus. 8 14 ܚܒܐ] nostri ܚܒܠ. 8 15 ܒܐܗܐ] nostri, ܒܗܘ. ibid. ܥܠ ܚܬܢܐ ܡܥ] Hebr. postulant ܡܥ ܚܬܢܐ ܥܠ sed libri non juvant. 8 16 ܠܡܕܥ] fortasse ܠܠܕܥ. 8 33 ܠܡܕܥ ܠܐ] nostri ܠܡܕܥ. 8 36 ܘܡܐܘܝܗܘܢ] Poc. ܘܝܗܘܒ. 91 ܠܗܒܝ] nostri ܠܗܠ male. Ib. ܘܣܬܢܒܝ nostri ܘܚܕܝܢܒܐ. ܗ pro ܘ. 97 ܣܝ] Poc. ܣܝܝܘ. ܘܐܚܬܥܒ. 98 ܘܥܘ] nostri, ܘܥܘܢ. 99 ܘܡܚܒܪܝ] videtur scribendum ܝ.ܡܒܢܘܒܪ, etsi libri non juvant. 103 ܚܟܝܡ] nostri ܚܟܝܡܐ ܘܒܐܝܗ. 104 ܘܚܟܝܡ] nostri, ܘܚܟܝܡܐ. 10 15 ܚܕܝܘܐܠܘ] Poc. ܚܕܝܘܐܠܘ. 10 18 ܠܡܒܝܢܝ] nostri, ܠܚܒܝܢܐ. 10 20 ܣܢܝܪ] nostri, ܣܢܝܪܘ.

The yield of this collation is negligible. While it is, of course, quite possible that a careful collation of all existing Mss. would help us to correct a number of inferior readings, it seems likely that most corruptions will be found in almost all of them, and that our method of correction cannot be simply that of selecting the best reading of the Mss. Fortunately, we have the original Hebrew text from which S. was translated and we are therefore very frequently in a position to remedy the mistakes of the S text by a careful comparison with MT and by pointing out how the Syriac which we now have has been corrupted by copyists from a Syriac text which corresponded more closely to MT.

Syriac copyists were just as careless and just as careful as other copyists. They frequently confused letters which looked similar to others. We find, e. g., the following confusions more or less frequently:

ܐ, ܬ.
ܒ, ܟ, ܡ, ܢ, ܦ, ܩ, ܪ.
ܘ, ܬ.
ܢ, ܝ, ܠ, ܪ, ܬ.
ܦ, ܬ.
ܠ, ܪ.
ܚ, ܪ, ܬ.
ܕ, ܪ, ܢ, ܝ, ܠ, ܬ.
ܡ, ܘ, ܪ.
ܬ, ܬ.

ܡ, ܣ.
ܢ, ܪ.
ܣ, ܬ, ܡ.
ܬ, ܬ.
ܦ, ܘ.
ܒ, ܘ.
ܝ, ܢ, ܪ, ܪ.
ܐ, ܣ.
ܬ, ܪ.

Keeping this in mind, I find that the Syriac text should be corrected in the following places:

Proposed Corrections of the Syriac Text.

Ch. 1. 8. ܠܝܘܡܐ] ܠܝܠܘܬܐ. — 11. ܐܡܪܝ] ܐܡܪܚ, cf. 5 14 same error.

Ch. 2. 2. ܠܡܠܠ] ܡܡܠܠ. — 12. ܐܪܡܝ] ܚܠܝܡ. — 17. ܐܪܘ] ܕܪܘ. — 18. ܠܝܘܡܐ] ܠܝܘܡ. — 19. ܠܣܡܡ] ܣܡܡ. — 20. ܠܚܡ] ܚܡܪ. — 25. ܡܝܡܡ] ܡܚܡܡܐ, ܡܪܡܐ ܠܐܡܚܐ [ܐܚܙܝ ܐܚܕ. — 30. ܡܝܚܡܡ, ܡܪܚܕܠܐ] ܣܪܡ. — 33. ܐܪܡܝ] ܣܪܡ. — 36. ܐܚܕܚ] ܐܡܪܚ. — 40. ܠܡܪܚܕܠܐ ܚܡܕܠ] ܚܡܕܠ, ܠܠܡܝ [ܠܠܡܚܝ, ܠܐܚܕܬܐ [ܐܚܕܬܐ. — 42. ܡܚܕܠܐ] ܡܚܬܢ. [ܐܪܘ] ܐܡܚܐ ܠܠܐ, ܠܡܚܐ [ܡܪܚܡ. — 44. ܣܡܡܠܐ [ܣܡܚܡܠ, ܠܠܦܠܐ] 43. ܠܐܠܚܡ [ܠܠܚܡ. — 45. ܠܠܚܡܡܗ [ܚܡܡܗ. — 47. ܠܠܚܡܚ] ܚܡܚ, ܠܡܚ [ܠܠܡܚ] ܠܐܠܚ. — 48. ܐܡܪܚ] ܐܪܚ, ܐܙܘܐܠ [ܐܘܣܝ. — 49. ܠܚܡܐ [ܣܡܡܡ, ܠܚܡܐ [ܚܡܐ. — 50. ܐܣܡܠܐ [ܐܡܐ ܠܡܐܠܠ] ܡܚܕܡܚܡ. — 51. ܐܣܘܣܝ] ܣܪܡܣܝ. — ܠܚܡܐ [ܣܡܚ. — 50.

INTRODUCTION 9

52. اسیرا [اسیرا or اسیرا, cf. text. ad. loc. — 53. مومومه] حرمومه, احد [احد. — 54. سلوما [سلیما (?). — 55. ححد [ححب, — رامعی [رامعی, علمم [صلمم. — 56. ححل [ححل, رامعی [احتمحلمر — 57. معلعل [ححب. احد [احد, ممرما [ممرما. — 58. معلمر [ححر — 59. ١لمعسلا [١لعدس, معادح [مرعد. — 60. لمعرا [لمعرا. — 61. رمععى [رمععر.
Ch. 3. 2. معلكاىا [علكاىا. — 8. ه‍ز [هر. — 9. مرمصا [مرمصا, ٣‍مرا [‍سمر. — 11. حمعددا [حمعددا.
Ch. 4. 6. سلمسا [صلمسا. — 7. محارا, ١مارا, cf. 18. — 8. هصعا — ١صمعر [١‍صعمر. — 10. ١ّدسا [١ّدسا, لرعدلا, لرعدلا. — 9. ‍حرعصا. — 22. لعدلا [لعدلقا.
Ch. 5. 3. ١محارحوررب [١محارحوررب. — 16. وا [حمدا, حبا ١ل١‍را (?).
Ch. 6. 2. رامرعا [رامرعا. — 3. رامرع [رامرع. — 4. ١‍١ّدحلا [مرددحلا (?). — 12. بحمر [بحمعر, ١محمی [و١محمی.
Ch. 7. 2. ح‍ب] حاب.
Ch. 8. 2. ١محر [١محر. — 4. ١لما مسلب حلب [١لمومحلنب. — 5. ١حرمعا [١حرمعا. — 7. ١محلعا [ححلحعا. — 8. ١ّرمرا [١ّرمرا. — 9. ١سارا [سارا. — 10. صمعا [مصمعصا. — 12. حلمی [حلمی, ١رمعا [ارمعا. — 13. بسمعمر [ارسمعمر, ‍ححاررا [‍ححاررا. — 15. ١حدا [١حدا, ١لمر [١لمر, ١لمدا [ح‍رب, حمررب [حمررب. — 18. رامرا [رامرا. — 16. ١لمرب [١لمرب. — 33. حىى [حلب‍ع (?). — 21. لحلمعحی [لحلمعحی. — حرعدلا.
Ch. 10. 2. سارا [سارا. — 6. ١لمعمد [١لمعمد. — 9. ا١لحصعرمر [١لحصعرمر or صححلب [صححلب, سالب [سالب, حصالب [حصالب. — 15. حعماىا [حعماىا, — 18. حححلب. — 18. حمررب [حمررب. — 21. سالب [سالب. — 22. ١لم] محلا ,١حرحم [١حرحم ,حعححالب [حعحلالب, ا١لمعدمر, ١لمعحم. — 23. ١حرحم [١حرحم. — 24. محلا ومه محلما [محلما. — ١واب [١اوب, ا١لمعحد [ا١لمعحد. — 25. لعلسا [لعلسا, حلسمعی [حلسمعی, صمعی [صمعی, ا١لحدار [ا١لحدار or ا١لعدار [ا١لعدار. — 26. لعلسا [لعلسا, ا١لمعحد, ١سسب [١سسب, ر١حلا [ر١حلا ١حلا. — 27. سالب or سالب [سالب, ا١حالرب [ا١حالرب, محلاسا [محلاسا, ا١لمعحد [ا١لمعحد, لعلسا [لعلسا, محلاسا [محلاسا, ر١حم [ر١حم, حاررا [حاررا. — 29. حمب [ا١لمعحد [ا١لمعحد, ١لمعحد [ا١لمعحد. — علالا [علالا, ١‍رمعد [١‍رمعد, حررحا [حررحا, حررحا, حلعالمر [حلعالمر. — 30. [١لععا. — 31. ححعمعا وصمعا, وحصلامب حلعد ‍صمعا, حررا [حرررا, ١‍مملا. — 32. حمب [حمب — 34. حلمعد [حلمعد, احم [حرمعد. — 33. صمررمعا [صمررمعا. — 32. ١رمعلا, — ‍حرررا [حرا١را. — 35. حر] حرمعا. — 37. حعمحل] ححعمعد. — 39. حلعالمر [حلعالمر (?).

] ܠܚܘܼܥܐ 43. — .ܚܪܙܐܝܠ] ܢܙܪܐܝܠ 41. — .ܗܢܒ]ܨܥܢ, ܡܕܡܪܬ] ܡܕܡܬ 40.
ܢܠܝܥ.

While most of these corrections concern names, there is still a goodly number of other cases where the original reading has been restored. It seems to me quite obvious that the method which Professor Bewer used in his "Text des Buches Ezra" for the Greek versions, must be applied to the Syraic text too and that any editing of S. which simply professes to give the best available text of the Mss. is not a critical edition. We are not left to speculate or to conjecture wildly about a possible text, because we have the Hebrew text from which S. was translated and have therefore a constant check and norm at our disposal. It is, of course, not claimed that every one of the above proposed emendations of S. represents certainly the original Syriac reading, but I believe in most cases it has actually been rediscovered by this method. This, in itself, is an important contribution to the textual history of the Book of Ezra, but it is not the most valuable, because it is even more significant that in our comparison of S. with MT we find a number of places where S. has retained a better reading than MT, in other words, where the *original Hebrew Text* can be restored on the basis of S.

Before giving a list of these, we must make clearer the character of the Peshitta Version of Ezra.

The Syriac translation, as has already been pointed out, is, in the main, carefully made and true to the sense without being slavishly literal. The translator has done exactly as we do in rendering French or German into English. On the other hand, in the forms of the verb, especially in the suffixes, and in the additions and omissions of the copula, a greater freedom is taken than we would like. How far this can be laid at the door of the copyists we cannot say.

In the matter of synonyms for theological ideas and offices an interchange is common; but in no case is the sense of the text injured. In the case of doublets, such as 9 7 und 10 12, the blame must not be laid on the translator. These are more likely marginal references which later copyists put into the text.

As is to be expected in any text that has suffered much at the hands of copyists, there are many words omitted. The omissions, however, are of an unimportant nature. They consist mostly of particles, the copula, words not understood, and certain words in paraphrastic phrases. Omissions occur in: 1 1, 2, 6; 2 31, 68, 69; 3 13; 4 3, 5, 10, 13, 14, 17, 22; 5 7, 8, 11, 12, 15, 17; 6 1, 2, 3, 5, 7, 8, 10, 13, 20, 21; 7 1, 9, 10, 12, 13, 14, 15, 17, 24, 28; 8 3, 6, 15, 20, 26, 27; 9 6, 8; 10 9, 14, 19, 20, 23, 24, 25, 27, 29, 30, 31, 43.

There is also a large number of additions. These, as in the case of the omissions, are of an unimportant character and are due to the copyists. By far the largest number of the omissions and additions are those of the copula. The translator has also a fondness for adding the obvious, *e. g.*, when a person is referred to in MT by name only, the S. translator adds, in nearly every case the title of his office, e. g., Ezra (the scribe or priest), etc. Additions occur in: 1 1, 2, 6, 7, 10, 11; 2 1, 3, 4, 5, 7, 11, 13, 14, 17, 19, 21, 23, 26, 27, 28, 31, 33, 36, 37, 41, 42, 58, 60, 62, 64, 65, 66, 67; 3 8, 9, 10, 12; 4 2, 3, 6, 7, 8, 12, 15, 17, 19, 23; 5 3, 8, 11, 14, 17; 6 3, 8, 9, 11, 14, 16, 18, 20, 21; 7 1, 6, 7, 10, 12, 13, 14, 15, 16, 18, 21, 23, 25, 27; 8 1, 17, 19, 26, 30; 9 1, 4, 5, 7, 10, 13, 15; 10 2, 3, 5, 6, 7, 8, 9, 10, 12, 13, 15, 16, 19, 30, 35, 41, 42.

Variants in the Divine name commonly occur. The translator invariably renders יהוה by ܡܪܝܐ in keeping with Jewish tradition. Occasionally אלהים is also rendered by ܡܪܝܐ *e. g.* 1 5; 3 8, 9; 6 22; 7 15; 10 1, 6, 9.

Words are sometimes misunderstood. Several words from the Persian occur in Ezra. These the translator has not always understood as is shown by the following: אספרנא which S. has as follows: 5 8 ܒܚܦܝܛܘ cf. note *ad loc.* 6 8 omits; 6 12 ܒܥܓܠ "quickly"; 7 21 ܒܚܦܝܛܘ "zealously"; 7 17, 26 ܒܛܝܒܘ "carefully". התרשתא, the designation of the Persian Governor of Judea in Ezra 2 63 is given as ܪܝܫ ܐܣܦܪܢܐ. Cf. note *ad loc.* In Ezra 4 13, 20; 7 24 is a list of the terms used for toll and customs. The translator misunderstood these terms and rendered as follows: 4 13, MT "tribute, custom, toll" by a paraphrase "there will be no tribute for thee". 4 20: Here the translator departs yet farther from MT, paraphrasing the original "and tribute, toll, and custom was paid them" by "and for the former kings they had no regard at all." 7 24, MT reads, "Tribute, custom, and toll it is not lawful to levy on them" by "it is not lawful to say a thing to them." In 4 8, 5 4, and 6 13 occurs the word כנמא which the translator mistook and translated by ܐܝܟ ܕܡܥܕ except in 5 9, 11, where the word occurs again it is correctly rendered. In 4 13 the word אפתם "impost" (reading with many Mss. אפתס) is incorrectly translated by ܐܦ ܗܝ "also she".

As to the k'thib and ḳ're the translator used his own judgment as to the better reading but preferred the ḳ're to the k'thib. Out of a total of 28 cases, the translator uses the ḳ're 17 times, the k'thib 6 times and follows his own judgment 5 times. The list follows:

	K'thib	Ḳ're	Syriac	
2 1	נבוכדנצור	נבוכדנצר	ܢܒܘܟܕܢܨܪ	= ḳ're.
2 46	שמלי	שלמי	ܫܠܡܝ	= ḳ're.
2 50	נפיסים	נפוסים	ܢܦܘܣܝܡ	= ḳ're.
3 3	ויעל	ויעלו	ܘܐܣܩܘ	= ḳ're.

INTRODUCTION

	K'thib	Ḳ're	Syriac
4 2	ולא	ולו	ܡܠܘܗܝ = ḳ're.
4 4	ומבלהים	ומבהלים	ܘܡܒܗܠܝܢ = k'thib.
4 7	כנותו	כנותיו	ܐܘܢܗ = k'thib.
4 9	ארכוי	ארכויא	ܐܚܪܐ S. here follows

neither k'thib nor ḳ're but reads independently ארכיא which a later scribe has carelessly written ארביא. Torrey suggests this reading[1] but gives no credit to the Peshitta.

4 9	דהוא	דהיא	ܗܝ = ḳ're.
4 11	עבדיך	עבדך	ܥܒܕܝܢ = k'thib.
5 1	נביאה	נביא	ܢܒܝܐ = ḳ're.
5 12	כסדיא	כסדאה	ܟܠܕܝܐ = ḳ're.
6 14	נביאה	נביא	ܢܒܝܐ = ḳ're.
6 17	לחטיא	לחטאה	ܬܚܠܦ = independent.
7 18	עליך	עלך	ܠܟ = ḳ're.
	אחיך	אחך	ܐܚܝܟ = k'thib.
7 25	דאנין	דינין	ܢܬܢܒ = ḳ're.

7 26 S. paraphrases and reads independently.

| 8 13 | יעואל | יעיאל | ܝܚܘܐܠ S. read originally |

ḳ're. A copyist has confused ܘ and ܝ.

| 8 14 | זבוד | זכור | ܙܒܘܕ = ḳ're. |

8 17 S. paraphrases but follows ḳ're *ad sensum*.

10 2	עולם	עילם	ܥܠܡ = ḳ're.
10 12	כדבריך	כדברך	ܐܝܟ ܦܬܓܡܟ = k'thib.
10 29	ירמות	ורמות	ܘܪܡܘܬ = k'thib.
10 35	כלוהי	כלוהו	ܟܠܗܘܢ = independent.
10 37	ויעשו	ויעשי	ܘܥܒܕ = ḳ're originally.
10 43	ידו	ידי	S. omits.
10 44	נשאי	נשאו	ܢܣܒܘ = ḳ're.

This proves that the translator knew the traditional reading of the synagogue but by no means felt bound by

---

[1] Cf. *Ezra Studies,* ad loc.

that system. No decisive argument can be deduced from the above to prove that the translator was a Jew; a Christian would have known the ḳ're corrections as well as a Jew.

Differences in vocalization frequently occur. The majority of these instances are confined to proper names. All these cases are fully discussed in the text further on.

Free paraphrases occur in every chapter. These are in some instances due to foreign words, the meaning of which the translator did not know. In the second place, the translator shows a predilection to add explanatory words, such as priest, prophet, etc. In the third case, paraphrases explain what would otherwise be unintelligible to the translator's readers. G. misunderstood some of these passages in the original and nothing, it would seem, shows so clearly the independence of S. over G as 2 63: MT כהן לאורים ולתמים (cf. Neh. 7 65). S. paraphrases by ܟܗܢܐ ܡܠܦ ܘܡܫܠܡ, while G^AB translates with an attempt at extreme literalness ἱερεὺς τοῖς φωτίζουσιν καὶ τελείοις which makes no sense. G^AB wrongly connects אורים and תמים with אור and תמם. The Peshitta translator understood the meaning. First, there is the addition of ܟܗܢܐ to ܡܠܦ (cf. Ex. 28 30, Lev. 8 18, Num. 27 21) which shows historical accuracy and also is in keeping with the translator's habit of adding explanatory words. In the second place, he paraphrases correctly the meaning of לאורים ולתמים. If the Peshitta translation of Ezra had been made under the influence of G, should we not expect its influence to be seen in a difficult passage such as this?

Another passage of the same order is 9 4 where מנחת הערב is translated by ܥܕ ܠܨܦܪܐ. Here again G^AB follows MT literally with τῆς θυσίας τῆς ἑσπερινῆς. The translator of the Peshitta, however, with historical accuracy, renders "until the ninth hour", *i. g.*, the hour of prayer, which, in the times, when there was no temple, and so no minḥah, took the place of the evening sacrifice[1]. The translator, exactly as in 2 63, has not literally rendered words which might be misunderstood or meaningless but by his paraphrase has made the passage perfectly intelligible to his readers.

Another instance occurs in 10 1. MT has here "and the people wept"; the translator has paraphased this as "the children wept" which seemed to him to be the true meaning of the original.

While these instances show the freedom of the translator, they by no means prove that the Peshitta is a mere paraphrase. Moreover, in none of these illustrations is there the slightest dependence on G. These passages and a few similar ones that occur in the translation are fully discussed in the comparison of the text with MT.

It is manifest that the Syriac translator has succeeded, on the whole, remarkably well in presenting the Book of Ezra in a good Syriac dress to his countrymen and that it could thus take its place appropriately in the Syriac Bible.

For the Biblical scholar, however, and especially for the textual critic, the greatest value of the Peshitta of Ezra lies in the fact that it has in forty-two instances preserved the original reading, and therefore it must be employed to reconstruct the Hebrew text of the Massorites. These original readings are as follows:

1 6 לבד] ܣܓܝ = לָרֹב = "very much" which is undoubtedly the original reading.

2 25 קרית עריס] ܩܘܪܝܬ ܢܚܒܝ which was originally ܢܚܒܝ = יערים. A scribe has carelessly written ܒ for ܝ both here and in Neh. 7 29. S. represents here (in the original)

---
[1] Duhm, *Die Psalmen*, to Ps. 141 2. Cf. also *Acts*, 3 1.

the correct reading. MT is due to carelessness. G^(AB) and Neh. 7 29 both bear witness with S. that MT must be corrected.

3 4 עלת] ܐܥܠܘ S. here with G and several Heb. mss. has preserved the plural and MT must be corrected accordingly.

3 9 יהודה] ܝܗܘܕܝܐ = הודיה. As 2 40 shows, S. has here preserved the correct form of this name.

3 10 ויעמידו] ܘܥܡܕܘ = ויעמדו. S. agrees with several Heb. Mss. and G, and undoubtedly represents the original.

3 12 את־הבית הראשון] ܗܢܐ ܒܝܬܐ ܒܐ ܚܘܒܗ ܪܒܐ S. alone of all the versions has here preserved the original reading, viz. "this house in its great honor". MT has lost the words "in its great honor", and must be corrected by supplying הרב בִּכְבֹדוֹ.

בשמחה] ܘܒܚܕܘܬܐ. S. reads the copula, as does Esd., which is the correct reading. MT must be changed to ובשמחה.

4 3 המלך כורש מלך־פרש] ܟܘܪܫ ܡܠܟܐ ܒܠܚܘܕ S. omits המלך (G and Esd. also). MT should be corrected accordingly, since "King Cyrus, King of Persia" is evidently redundant.

4 10 בקריה] ܒܩܘܪܝܐ S. reads "in the cities of the province of Samaria". This (cf. 2 Kgs. 17 24) is also G's reading and is preferable to MT's "in the city".

4 23 רחום] + ܒܥܠ ܛܥܡܐ S. and G^L alone preserve the original text. The title בעל־טעם must be inserted in the Hebrew. Cf. vss. 8, 9, 17.

5 1 נביאיא] ܢܒܝܐ. S. has quite grammatically "Haggai the prophet and Zechariah the son of Iddo the prophet." This is certainly better than MT and it may represent the original text. The alternative is to follow Esd. in omitting נביאה after חגי.

5 4 אמרנא] ܐܡܪܘ. S. and G have preserved here the original text. MT must be emended to read אמרו.

5 17 בבבל די תמה די־מלכא גנזיא [בבית ܒܝܬ ܓܢܙܐ ܐܝܟܐ ܕܚܕܪܐ, ܘܡܠܟܐ, MT reads here "in the king's treasury there which is in Babylon" but S. reads "in the records, that are in the treasury of the kings of Babylon." MT does not here present the original text and must be emended to read with S. which here undoubtedly presents the original = בבית די בספריא גנזיא די מלכיא די בבל.

[דך ܕܝܢ, = די. So also several Heb. mss. and Esd. This is clearly the preferable reading. G has both readings.

6 2 [באחמתא ܚܠܣܥܐ. S. preserves the original form of this Persian word. Cf. BDB.

6 3 [בירושלם ܒܐܘܪܗܠܡ ܐܝܟܐ, = די־בירושלם. So several Heb. mss., Esd., G, and Vulg. This is the original text and MT must be corrected accordingly.

[שתין ܚܡܫܝܢ. S. corresponds here to 1 Kg. 6 2 and apparently represents the original. The reading in MT is influenced by the preceding שתין.

6 18 [על־עבידת אלהא ܒܝܬ ܐܠܗܐ, ܘܠܐܘܐ ܩܕܡ ܐܠܗܐ. S. agrees with G^L and is better than MT. We must insert therefore in the Aramaic text בית before אלהא.

7 12 [גמיר ܫܠܡ. S. alone has preserved the epistolatory style demanded, viz. "greeting".

7 19 [אלה ירושלם ܐܠܗܐ ܕܐܘܪܗܠܡ. S. presents the original and only possible reading. The reading in MT is unparalleled. MT must accordingly be corrected to אלהא די בירושלם.

7 22 [ועד בתין משח ܚܛܐ ܠܡܫܚܐ ܐܝܟ ܕܕܢ. The order of MT has been confused by a copyist and should read as does S. ועד משח בתין.

7 25 [דתי ܢܡܘܣܐ. S. translates by a singular. The Greek versions also have the singular which Guthe (Esra *ad loc*) and others believe is the original reading. Vs. 26 favors the singular = דָּת.

8 12 עשרה] ܚܡܫ. S. reads with 38 Heb. mss. and Esd.L what is undoubtedly the original. MT should be emended accordingly to עשרים.

8 24 חשביה] ܘܠܚܫܒܝܐ. S. with Esd.AB has preserved the original reading because Hashabia was not a priest but a Levite according to vs. 18.

8 34 במשקל] ܘܒܡܬܩܠܐ. The copula must be inserted in MT to read ובמשקל with S.

9 1 כתעבתיהם] ܒܛܢܦܘܬܗܘܢ = בתעבתיהם, so also G and this was most probably the original reading. So Bewer.

9 3 בגדי] ܠܒܘܫܝ. MT must be emended to read בגדי with S. instead of sing.

9 4 בדברי] ܡܠܬܐ ܕ = בדבר. The reading in S. is vouched for by G, Esd., and Vulg. and doubtlessly represents the original reading. Cf. Bewer ad loc.

9 12 עולם] ܥܠܡ = עילם = K're of MT which is preferable to MT kethib. This reading is vouched for by G, Esd.L and Vulg.

10 5 הלוים] ܘܠܘܝܐ. S. reads "priests and Levites" = והלוים MT should be corrected accordingly.

10 6 וילך] ܘܠܢ = וילן. A scribe has carelessly written ך for ן in MT. S, preserves the original reading. (Esd. also.)

10 7 וירושלם] ܘܠܐܘܪܫܠܡ. S. here has preserved the original which is vouched for by many Heb. Mss. and also by G. The context also demands it in agreement with the previous "in Judea".

10 14 עד] ܥܠ. MT must be emended to read על for עד according to the more original reading of S.

10 16 ויבדלו] ܘܦܪܫ. S. (cf. also G) gives evidence of an original וַיַּבְדֵּל which MT demands as Ezra is subject of the sentence. MT reads plural; but this must be emended.

10 16 לדריוש] ܠܡܒܚܫܘ ܒ = לדרוש. This is the correct reading. MT must be accordingly corrected.

INTRODUCTION 19

10 17 אנשים] ܣܠܝ̈ܐ ܚܪ̈ܐ. MT must be emended to read האנשים.

10 20 וזבדיה] ܙܒܕܝܠ. S. and 9 Heb. Mss. may well represent the original.

10 31 ‏[ובני חָרָם ܥܡ ܚܢܒ ܣܝܡ. G^{AB} and many Heb. mss. agree with S. in this reading which is doubtless original. MT must be corrected to read וּמִבְּנֵי. G^{AB}, Esd.^{ALB} vocalize חָרָם as does S. MT must also be corrected to read with S.

10 34 ‏[בני ܚܒܒ. Cf. vs. 29 where the "sons of Bani" are already listed. S. must be correct, as one clan would not be listed twice. MT must accordingly be corrected to read בכי.

‏[אואל ܣܐܠ = יוֹאֵל to which Esd.^{ABL} and G^{LB} also testify. MT must be accordingly corrected.

10 35 כלוהי, k're ‏[כלוהו ܡܠܝܗܘ = כליהו which may have preserved the original reading.

10 38 ‏[ובני ובנוי ܘܚܢܒ ܚܢܒܝ̈. S., in spite of a scribal corruption, has preserved the original reading ܘܚܢܒ ܚܒܘܝ, i. e. "the sons of Binnui". So also G. MT must be accordingly corrected to ובני בנוי.

2*

CHAPTER I

1. ירמיה] + ܢܒܝܐ. Cf. also 1 2, 7. The translator of Ezra adds such explanatory words. Cf. the parallel in 2 Chr. 36 22 where the same addition is made.

מפי] ܦܘܡܗ ܡܢ is a free translation. S. supports MT over against בפי of Esd. and G^L. In the duplicate section, 2 Chr. 36 22, בפי = ܡܢ ܦܘܡܗ.

כרש מלך פרס]. S. omits. כרש here, either by accident or by oversight of a copyist.

2. כל ממלכות] ܡܠܟܘܬܐ. The translator or a copyist may have omitted accidentally both כל and the s^ejāmē points of ܡܠܟܘܬܐ. But it is also possible that כל seemed superfluous to the translator, because he took the Hebrew to mean "the rule of the earth". In any case we need not assume that the translator had a Hebrew original different from the MT.

בירושלם] + ܐܘܪܫܠܡ. Cf. note on vs. 1.

3. מכל־עמו] ܡܢ ܥܡܗ ܟܠܗ. As in 2 Chr. 36 23 the duplicate section.

יהי] ܢܗܘܐ.

4. ינשאוהו] ܢܣܡܟܘܢܝܗܝ. This is a very literal translation which does not represent the true meaning of the Hebrew here which is to "help". G also did not know this meaning, translating λήμψονται.

5. לכל] ܟܠ.

יהוה] ܠܐܠܗܐ ܡܪܝܐ. The translator took the relative אשר to

refer to יהוה and translated "a house for the Lord יהוה *the God who* is in Jerusalem". Taking יהוה as a proper name, his addition, the God, was appropriate and quite in accordance with his habit (cf. note on 1 1). MT reads: "the house of יהוה which is in Jerusalem."

6. חוקו] ܐܣܪ. S. renders freely, due perhaps to בידיהם.

בזהב] ܘܣܐܒܐ etc. The translator does not repeat the preposition governing two nouns in succession as the Syriac style does not require such a repetition.

לבד] ܣܓܝ. MT here is evidently corrupt. S. (also Esd.) reads „very much" which is doubtless the original reading.

על־כל־התנדב] ܥܠ ܐܝܠܝܢ ܕܐܬܢܕܒ. S. understood התנדב as referring to the persons who gave freely and translated accordingly. MT took it as referring to the gifts which were given to the temple (in accordance with vs. 4) and its meaning is "in addition (על) to all that had been freely given" (to the temple). S's original apparently did not have כל, it was neither in G nor in Esd.L and must therefore have been omitted in the Hebrew mss. (accidentally through haplography). That it was in the older texts is clear not only from MT but from Esd.AB. Cf. Bewer, *Text des Buches Ezra*, S. 14.

7. נבוכדנצר] + ܡܠܟܐ ܕܒܒܠ. Cf. note on vs. 1.

8. מתרדת] ܡܗܕܬ. It is quite apparent that this reading is not due to the original translator who wrote ܡܬܪܕܬ but to a careless copyist who mistook ܪ for ܗ.

ששבצר] ܣܣܒܪܝ. This also must not be put to the account of the translator who wrote ܣܣܒܨܪ but to that of a careless scribe who wrote this incorrectly and fixed the wrong form in his mind, for he makes the same mistake in 1 11, 5 14.

9. אגרטלי] ܟܣܐ. S. interprets as meaning "bowls". מחלפים] ܫܚܠܦܐ. The translator connected the word with חלף *change*.

Cf. חליפה *garment for changing*. The Vulg. renders *cultri* and Esd. ϑυίσκαι ἀργυραῖ.

10. Apparently the translator had omitted the gold bowls first; then he noticed his mistake and added them with ܘܗܝ.

כלים] + ܘ. The addition of the copula, although of no critical significance, is noted. (Cf. discussion of these additions and omissions in the Introduction.)

11. ששבצר] ܫܫܒܨܪ. Cf. note on vs. 8.

ܡܚܕܬܐ ܕܣܠܩܐ ܡܢ ܓܠܘܬܐ [הגולה מבבל. The addition of ܕܣܠܩܐ is simply in the interest of a good translation.

CHAPTER II

1. מֹשְׁבֵי הַגּוֹלָה] ܣ. ܣܒܝ. The translator probably regarded הגולה as superfluous and, accordingly, left it untranslated. Cf. Neh. 7 6 where both words are literally rendered as in MT.

ܗܓܠ,. . . . ܐܘܒܠ ܐܢܘܢ ܠܒܒܠ [הַגְלָה . . . לְבָבֶל. S. freely renders MT's „carried into exile—to Babylon", by "which he carried into exile—and brought them to Babylon". Neh. 7 6 translates MT literally as above.

ܘܝܬܒܘ . . . ܐܬܘ [וַיָּשׁוּבוּ. This is a similar free translation.

2. וְזְרֻבָּבֶל] ܘܙܘܪܒܒܠ. This is the regular Syriac vocalization in Ezra, Neh., Hag., and Zech.

בִּלְשָׁן] ܒܠܣܡ. This is due to a different vocalization.

מִסְפָּר] ܡܢܝܢ. The translator misunderstood this name and incorrectly translated it "number".

אַנְשֵׁי עַם יִשְׂרָאֵל] ܐܢܫܐ ܕܐܝܣܪܐܝܠ. S. avoids the tautological expression of MT by omitting עַם. In Neh. 7 7, however, S. translates it verbatim.

6. פַּחַת מוֹאָב] ܦܚܬ ܡܘܐܒ in Ezra. S. always translates פחת as if it were a noun. (Neh. 7 11 idem.) The translator of Hag. 1 1, 2 22 renders it by ܪܒܐ, taking it as did the translator of Ezra. The term had, by this time, become a proper name.

לִבְנֵי] ܒܢܝ. S. disregards the לְ = "namely" (cf. 1 5) and continues the catalogue noting each as a separate clan.

24   A CRITICAL EXAMINATION OF THE PESHITTA

ויואב [יואב‎ ܘܝܘܐܒ. S correctly renders ויואב. Neh. 7, and Esd. also vouch for the reading in S.

8. ותוא] ܠܠܝ. The difference in the vocalization is probably due to the omission of the *mater lectionis* in the Ms. which the translator used.

10. שש] was omitted by a careless scribe.

12. עזגד] ܚܪܡܝ. This is evidently a scribal corruption for ܚܪܓܝ. Cf. Neh. 7 17.

13. אדניקם] ܐܕܘܢܝܩܡ. This is the usual Syriac transcription. Neh. 7 17 and Ezra 8 13 ܐܕܘܢܣܡ is a scribal corruption for ܐܕܘܢܝܩܡ.

15. עדין] ܚܪܝܢ. This is the same as in Neh. 7 20. Cf. note on 2 8.

חמשים] ܘܐܠܦ. This mistake was probably occasioned by the figure in the preceding verse.

16. ליחזקיה] ܠܚܙܩܝܐ. This is without ו preformative as MT Neh. 7 21.

17. בצי] ܒܨܝ. This is a copyist's mistake for the original ܒܨܝ as in Neh. 7 23.

18. יורה] ܝܘܪܐ. Misled by a confusion of ܘ and ܪ, a scribe thought the well known ܝܘܪܐ was meant and wrote accordingly. There is no reason to think that this corresponded to a different Heb. original.

19. חשם] ܚܫܘܡ. Note the different vocalization. Neh. 7 22 is a scribal error for ܚܫܘܡ.

20. גבר] ܓܒܥ is partly due to the confusion of ܘ and ܪ and partly to the careless omission of ܒ. As in 2 18 it is not necessary to hypothecate a different Heb. original.

22. נטפה] ܢܛܘܦܐ. This vocalization, as in Neh. 7 26 is due to the absence of the *mater lectionis* in the translator's Heb. Ms.

25. קרית ערים] ܩܘܪܝܬ ܥܕܝܢ. This was originally ܥܪܝܢ. A scribe has carelessly written ܕ for ܪ both here and in Neh. 7 29.

S. presents here (in the original) the correct reading. MT's reading is due to carelessness. G^AB and Neh. 7 29 both bear witness with 2 25 that MT must here be corrected.

ובארות שבע]. The printed Syriac texts here have a wrong division of these words as ܘܒܐܪܘܬ.ܫܒܥ which were originally, of course, ܘܒܐܪܘܬ ܫܒܥ as Neh. 7 29. Thorndyke's Mss. read this also.

26. שש מאות] ܫܬܡܐܐ. This is a scribal error due to the preceding verse. Cf. vss. 10, 15, and Neh. 7 30.

28. והעי] ܘܥܝ. S. omits the article in proper names as do the English versions.

30. מגביש] ܡܓܒܝܫ. This is due to a scribal confusion of ܒ and ܘ.

31. אחר]. S. omits.

33. חדיד] ܚܪܝܕ. This mistake of ܘ and ܝ is due to a copyist.

ואונו] ܘܐܘܢܐ. This is as Neh. 7 37; the difference is due to a copyist.

37. אִמֵּר] ܐܡܪ. S. writes as in 7 40 with different vocalization, but in 1. Chr. 9 12, 24 14, ܐܡܪ.

אלף] + ܣܠܦ. This addition is due to the influence of the following verse.

38. ארבעים ושבעה] ܡܐܬܝܢ ܘܐܪܒܥܝܢ. This is due to carelessness.

39. חרם] ܚܪܝܡ. S. writes with a different vocalization. Cf. vss. 15, 22, 30.

40. וקדמיאל] ܘܩܕܡܐܠ. The omission of ܠ here is due to the carelessness of a scribe. In Neh. 7 43 this word is correctly written.

לבני] ܠܒܢܝ. Both MT and S. are here corrupt. The original Heb. had the proper name וּבְנוּי. Cf. vs. 6.

הודויה] ܗܘܕܝܐ = הודיה. S. agrees here with the k're of Neh. 7 43. (So also in 3 9.)

41. המשרתים] ܡܫܡܫܢܐ = המשרתים. MT is correct.

26 A CRITICAL EXAMINATION OF THE PESHITTA

42. הַשְּׁעָרִים] ܬܪܥܐ. This is a copyist's error for ܬܪܥܐ. Cf. vs. 40 for opposite mistake in writing final ܢ. The translator took this word for a proper name. This accounts for the addition of the copula to the following ܗܘ.

טַלְמוֹן] ܐܠܡܢ. This is due to a copyist's interchanging of letters.

עֲקוּב] ܚܩܘܒ. As in Neh. 7 45, the copyist's error is due to dittography. The mistake was easily made, as יַעֲקֹב is a more familiar name than עַקּוּב.

חֲטִיטָא] ܚܛܝܛܐ. S. writes the word with different vocalization.

43. צִיחָא] ܨܝܚܐ. This is evidently a copyist's error for the original ܨܝܚܐ as in careless writing they look so much alike. Cf. Neh. 7 45 where ܨܝܚܐ occurs.

חֲשׂוּפָא] ܚܣܘܦܐ. S. writes with a different vocalization. Cf. 2 42. The confusion of ܣ and ܫ is due to a copyist.

44. סִיעֲהָא] ܣܥܐ. This is a copyist's error for the original ܣܥܕܐ.

קֶרֶס] ܩܪܣ. This is the result of a copyist's confusion of ܪ and ܕ.

פָּדוֹן] ܦܪܘܢ. This is the result of a copyist's confusion of ܪ and ܕ.

45. לְבָנָה] ܠܒܢܐ. This is evidently a copyist's error for the original ܠܒܢܐ and is due to a confusion of ܘ and ܢ.

עֲקוּב] ܚܩܘܒ. Cf. vs. 42 for the same confusion of ܣ and ܫ.

46. שַׂמְלַי] ܫܡܠܝ. So also MT k̇'re and Neh. 7 48.

47. גָּדֵל] ܓܕܠ. This is the result of copyist's confusion of ܕ and ܪ.

נְחַר] ܢܚܪ. As in Neh. 7 49, this transposition of consonants is due to a copyist.

רְאָיָה] ܪܥܝܐ. This is due to a copyist's confusion of ܪ and ܕ. Cf. the worse confusion in Neh. 7 50, ܪܥܐ for ܪܥܝܐ.

48. רְצִין] ܪܨܝܢ. As in Neh. 7 50, the ܨ is a copyist's error, but the punctation is truly Aramaic.

VERSION OF THE BOOK OF EZRA 27

‎[נקודא] ܢܩܘܕܐ. Here is a confusion of ܀ and ܂, as well as of ܘ and ܗ, with a good Semitic name as the result. In Neh. 7 50 the name appears as ܢܩܘܕܐ.

49. ‎[פסח] ܦܣܚ. This is due to a confusion of ܣ with ܠ.
‎[בסי] ܒܣܝ. This is due to a confusion of ܝ with ܘ.

50. ‎[אסנה] ܐܣܢܐ. This is due to a confusion of ܀ with ܘ.
‎[מעונים] ܡܥܘܢܝ. This is due to a confusion of ܣ with ܡ.
‎[נפיסים] ܢܦܝܣܝ. S. reads as does MT ḳ're.

51. ‎[חרחור] ܚܪܚܘܪ. This is due to a confusion of ܂ with ܃.
Cf. Neh. 7 53 where ܚܪܚܘܪ is due to an aural error.

52. ‎[מחידא] ܡܚܝܕܐ. This is probably due to a confusion of ܝ with ܂; but several Heb. mss. read מחירא both here and in Neh. 7 54.

53. ‎[ברקום] ܒܪܩܘܡ. This is due to a confusion of ܘ with ܗ.
‎[תמח] ܬܡܚ. As in Neh. 7 56, this is due to the careless writing of a scribe.

54. ‎[חטיפא] ܚܛܝܦܐ. This is due to a different vocalization which G^B also has.

55. ‎[עבדי] ܥܒܕܝ. This is due to the omission of ܘ and the confusion of ܂ with ܃.
‎[שלמה] ܫܠܡܐ. The ܚܢ is a mistake. The translator took עבדי and שלמה as two names as in vs. 58. Neh. 7 60 S. = MT. = ܥܒܕܝ ܫܠܡܐ.
‎[סטי] ܣܛܝ. The ܣ is due to the preceding ܫܠܡܐ.
‎[הספרת] ܗܣܦܪܬ. This is due to a different vocalization.

56. ‎[יעלה] ܝܥܠܐ. The ܠ is omitted by haplography as in Neh. 7 58 and ܝܥܠܐ comes from vs. 57.
‎[דרקון] ܕܪܩܘܢ. The ܐ is a copyist's error for ܘ.

57. ‎[בני שפטיה] is omitted here and transposed to vs. 56.
‎[חטיל] ܚܛܝܠ. This is due to a different vocalization.
‎[פכרת] ܦܟܪܬ. This is due to a confusion of ܘ and ܗ and to a different vocalization.
‎[הצבים] ܗܨܒܝܡ. The translator took הצ״ not as a name

but as a noun and wrongly connected it with צבא whose plural is צבאות. Neh. 7 59 ܚܢܒ ܘܚܒ; G^B υἱοὶ Ἀσεβωείν; G^A omits and reads: υἱοί, and as usual translates literally.

אמר] ܐܡܪ is a copyist's error for original ܐܡܪ.

58. עבדי שלמה] ܚܒܪ ܘܥܒܕܘ. Cf. note on vs. 55. The translator wrongly takes as two separate names.

59. תל מלח] ܠܬܠܡܣܚ. This is due to a transposition of consonants.

תל חרשא] ܠܬܠܚܒܐ. The translator mistook these words and prefixed ܠ = place to which; then took חַרְשָׁא as the Aramaic word חֻרְשָׁא for "forest" = ܚܒܐ, together making ܠܬܠܚܒܐ to "Tel-'Aba". Evidently the translator knew nothing of the geography of this region.

כרוב] ܘܠܟܪܘܒܐ. Again the translator takes this as a place to which and prefixed ܠ as well as the copula "and". He reads a different vocalization and a scribe has added ܂ making what, to him, was a familiar name.

אדן אמר] ("(from) Addan, Immer") ܐܕܝܢ ܐܬܚܘܝ] "then it was reported". As in Neh. 7 61, S. takes these names for a clause. The mistake was easy to make as the translator thought in Aramaic and when his eye caught these words he carelessly translated as above. Cf. his careless translation of מספר in vs. 2.

אם] ܐܠܐ ܂ܕ. S. translates MT's "whether" by "except that (they were of Israel)." In MT it is questionable whether these Exiles were of the stock of Israel; in S. the only question is their ability to show a certificate of birth.

60. נקודא] ܒܥܒܝܕ. This is due to a scribe's confusion of ܘ and ܝ and to a different vocalization.

61. ומבני הכהנים]. S. omits.

הקוץ] ܩܘܣ. A copyist has carelessly transposed the consonants.

62. נמצאו] ܐܫܬܟܚܘ = מצאו.

כתבם המתיחשים] ܟܬܒܐ ܕܝܚܣܝܗܘܢ. Here are free but good translations, and, in no way, presuppose a different Hebrew original.

63. התרשתא] ܐܢܫܐ ܕܐܬܪܫܡܘ. This is an unsuccessful attempt to explain a Persian word (tiršatha) which the translator did not know. More than 700 years intervened between Ezra and the translator and the Persian terms for office were entirely unknown to him. The plural form of the verb is necessited by ܐܢܫܐ. Cf. Neh. 7 65 where this word is rendered ܡܥܫܢܐ ܕܡܕܝܢܬܐ.

כהן] ܟܘܡܪܐ ܪܒܐ. Here, as in Esd., "the high priest" is an interpretative translation.

לאורים ולתומים] ܘܢܫܐܠ ܘܢܚܙܐ "and he shall inquire and determine (lit. see)". Here a paraphrase of the terms Urim and Thummim is given by the translator as the original significance of these terms was unknown to the popular reader.

65. MT ולהם משררים ומשררות] "and their singers male and female". S. ܘܡܫܡܫܢܝܗܘܢ ܕܡܫܡܫܝܢ ܠܗܘܢ "and their servants who were serving them . . . . ." This mistake arose from the similarity of the words משררים and משרתים.

68. התנדבו לבית האלהים להעמידו על־מקומו = they gave free will offerings for the house of God to establish it upon its site. S. ܐܬܡܠܟܘ ܠܒܝܬܐ ܕܡܪܝܐ. ܘܩܡܘ ܘܗܘܘ ܚܣܝܢܐܝܬ = they planned together for the house of the Lord; and then rose up and did bravely. S. paraphrases here but not correctly.

האלהים] ܡܪܝܐ Cf. 1 5, 3 8, 9.

69. דרכמונים] ܕܪܝܟܘܢܐ. S. gives the Persian equivalent.

שש] ܫܬܐ is less usual than ܫܬ.

וכסף]. S. omits ܘ before ܟܣܦܐ.

70. וַיֵּשְׁבוּ] ܘܝܬܒܘ. The *matres lectionis* not appearing in the ms., our translator read וַיֵּשְׁבוּ; then he added ܡܢ to the words "singers and porters".

30 A CRITICAL EXAMINATION OF THE PESHITTA

בעריהם] ܘܥܡܘܪ̈ܝܗܘܢ. The ܘ is evidently a mistake for ܒ.

[ܘ̣ܗܦܟ ܠܠܗ̇ ,ܘܗܘܘ +]. A comparison of MT und S. shows in translation the following:

MT.	S.
"The priests and levites, and (the rest) of the people, and the singers, and porters and the Nethinim dwelt in their cities, even all Israel *in their cities.*"[1]	"So the priests and levites and a part of the people and part of the servants and part of the porters and the Nethinim and those who were dwelling in their cities returned; and all Israel *in their cities.*"[1]

MT is certainly corrupt as it stands. S. tried to remedy the reading with the above result.

[1] Dittography. (S. corrected as above.)

CHAPTER III

1. ܠܥܡܐ ܠܐܘܪܫܠܡ [אל־ירושלם. MT has the people already at Jerusalem. In S. the people gather at some undefined place "to go up to Jerusalem". This does not imply that S. had a Heb. original different from that of our MT. S. presents here simply a paraphrastic element in the translation.

2. ܠܐܓܐܠ [שאלתיאל. S's reading is a copyist's mistake for ܐܠܬܐܠ. Cf. 3 8, 5 2 for a similar error.

ܢܒܝܐ ܕܐܠܗܐ [איש־האלהים. As in I Chr. 23 14 und II Chr. 30 16 S. renders the MT "man of God" by "prophet of God". Cf. Dt. 33 1 und Jos. 14 6 where the same phrase is rendered in S. by ܓܒܪܗ ܕܐܠܗܐ.

3. ܘܐܬܬܩܢ ܡܕܒܚܐ [ויכינו המזבח. S. translated freely by a passive.

ܐܣܬܐ [באימה. S. brings out the force of the strong אמה but disregards the preposition ב.

ܥܡܡܐ ܕܐܪܥܬܐ [הארצות. S. gives a correct paraphrastic translation.

ܥܠܬܐ [עלות לבקר. S. has the singular; but whether this is due to the translator or to a copyist who altered the pl. ܥܠܘܬܐ by carelessly copying, we do not know.

4. [עלת ܥܠܘܬܐ. Cf. vs. 3. Here S., the Greek versions and several Heb. mss. have the plural. This seems to be preferable.

6. [עלות ܥܠܘܬܐ. Cf. on vs. 3.

לא יסד] ܒܪܡܐ ܠܗܝܟܠܐ ܠܐ ܐܫܬܟܠܠ. Mt represents the temple as not yet begun, "the foundation was not laid;" S. represents the work as "not yet completed".

7. לצדנים ולצרים] ܠܨܘܪܝܐ ܘܠܨܝܕܢܝܐ. S. transposes the order.

אל־ים יפוא] ܒܝܡܐ ܠܝܘܦܐ. S. translates "by the sea to Joppa" freely but well. Cf. II Chr. 2 15.

8. האלהים] ܕܐܠܗܐ. Cf. 1 5, 2 68.

לירושלם] ܕܠܐܘܪܫܠܡ. Cf. 1 3, 4.

החלו] ܫܪܝ. S. is obviously an error for the original ܫܪܘ = MT. The ܪ was confused with ܕ and then to make a Syriac word ܪ was added.

הכהנים] ܘܟܘܡܪܐ. The addition of ܘ is due to a misunderstanding of S.

לנצח] ܠܡܗܘܐ ܒܝܘܡܐ. In rendering the Mt "to superintend" by "to be by the day", the translator wrongly reads for לְנַצֵּחַ which, in the unpointed text, was written with the same radicals, viz: לָנֶצַח "in perpetuo", "daily".

9. בניו ואחיו] ܘܐܚܘܗܝ ܘܒܢܘܗܝ. S. changes the order as in vs. 7.

קדמיאל] ܘܩܕܡܝܐ. This is due to a careless scribe who omitted the final ܠ as in 2 40.

בני יהודה] ܘܒܢܝ ܗܘܕܐ. S. has preserved this name better than MT. Cf. 2 40.

לנצח על־עשה] ܕܗܘܘ ܥܒܕܝܢ. S. translates MT "to superinted the doing (of the work)" by "who were doing" because of his misunderstanding לנצח in vs. 8.

בבית] ܕܒܝܬܗ. This is merely a free translation.

האלהים] ܕܐܠܗܐ. Cf. 1 5, 2 68, 3 8.

חנדד] ܗܢܕܪ. The confusion of ܕ and ܪ is due to a copyist; but the interchange of ה and ח doubtless goes back to the translator.

10. הבנים] ܕܒܢܝܐ. The MT "the builders" is rendered in S. "of the building". This is not correct. One might think

the original read ܘܚܢܐ = MT; but this would involve the change of position of ܚܢܐ which should come directly after ܘܐܚܘܗܝ.

וַיַּעֲמִידוּ [וַיַּעֲמִידוּ] ܘܩܡܘ. S. translates MT "and they stationed" by "and they rose up". S's reading (וַיַּעַמְדוּ) agrees with several Heb. Mss. as well as with the Greek versions and doubtlessly represents the original.

בחצצרות [בחצצרות] ܘܐܚܝܕܝܢ ܩܪܢܬܐ ܕܕܟܪܐ ܘܩܥܝܢ ܒܗܘܢ. S. here freely renders MT's "with trumpets" by "and holding rams' horns and blowing them".

במצלתים [במצלתים] ܒܨܨ̈ܠܐ. S. renders the MT's "with trumpets" by "with cymbals". But S. hardly had a different Heb. original. Cf. proceeding note.

11. ויענו בהלל ובהודה [ויענו בהלל ובהודה] ܘܫܒܚܘܗܝ ܘܐܘܕܝܘ. S. renders freely but well.

תרועה [תרועה] ܚܕܘܬܐ. This is a mistake in Lee's text for ܚܕܘܬܐ (Walton).

הוסד [הוסד] ܐܫܬܟܠܠ. True to the idea expressed in vs. 6, MT's laying of the foundation of the temple is S's "completion" of the same.

12. וראשי [וראשי] ܪ̈ܫܝ. S. carelessly omits the copula.

את־הבית הראשון ביסדו [את־הבית הראשון ביסדו] ܠܒܝܬܐ ܗܘ ܒܐܝܩܪܗ ܩܕܡܝܐ. S. renders MT's "the first house, when its foundation was laid" by "this house in its great former honor" (= בִּכְבֹדוֹ); and probably has alone of all the versions preserved an original reading. Cf. Bewer p. 46.

ביסדו [ביסדו] ܥܡ ܣܓܝ̈ܐܐ. Cf. vs. 11.

בשמחה [בשמחה] ܘܒܚܕܘܬܐ. S. reads the copula with Esd. which is the correct reading. MT should be changed to read ובשמחה accordingly.

13. השמחה [השמחה]. This is omitted by S. through oversight.

ܩܠܐ ،ܚܒܠܐ [והקול. Cf. translation of MT and S. following:

MT	S.
"And the people could not distinguish the sound of the shout of joy from the sound of the people's weeping; because the people were shouting a great shout and the sound was heard for a long distance."	"And the people could not hear the sound of the trumpets, because the people were blowing the trumpets with a loud noise, and the sound of weeping was heard for a long distance."

Both MT and S. are confused because the Hebrew is corrupt.

CHAPTER IV

2. נבנה] ܢܒܢܐ ܐܦ ܣܒ. S. brings out the meaning freely but correctly by rendering "we also will build".

נדרוש] ܢܒܢܐ. S. repeats "we will build"; but this a copyist's error for ܢܒܥܐ = נדרוש.

ܢܠܗ̈ܘ ܘܕܒܚܝܢ, ܗܦܐ ܘܠܐ]ולא אנחנו זבחים. S. had the same reading as Ḳ're, i. e. וְלוֹ for ולא and freely and pointedly adds "here," evidently meaning these "enemies" also had been in the habit of worshipping Jahweh *at Jerusalem.*

אסרחדן] ܣܢܚܪܝܒ. This reading of "Sennacherib" for "Esarhaddon" by no means makes the presupposition of a different underlying text necessary. Sennacherib, the father of Esarhaddon, was more familiar to the translator than his son, and the misreading may therefore have been quite accidental.

3. ܠܗܐ]. S. freely adds. Cf. note on 1 1.

המלך]. S. omits as does G. and Esd.: MT should be corrected accordingly; for "king Cyrus king of Persia" is evidently redundant.

4. עם הארץ] ܚܦ̈ܡܐ. The MT "people of the land", *i. e. common* people, seems always to denote a contrast with Israel, "the chosen people". Originally the phrase meant *the native races of Palestine* and later *the heathen.* The irony of MT is lost by S. which freely renders "peoples". Cf. 3 4 where this phrase is also paraphrased. 9 1 shows

clearly the significance of the phrase as meaning "heathen"; S. here renders "people of the provinces" which brings out the exact meaning.

לבנות] ܕܠܐ ܢܒܢܘܢ. This is a free but good translation.

5. יועצים] ܡܣܟܘ̈ܢܐ. This is evidently a copyist's error in S. for the original ܡܠܟܘܢܐ = יֹעֲצִים. Thorndyke in Walton suggests ܡܠܟܘ̈ܢܐ.

ועד] ܥܕܡܐ, without the copula.

6. אחשורוש] ܐܚܫܝܪܫ ܡܠܟܐ. Cf. note on 1 1.

שטנה] ܫܛܢܐ. In the sense of accusation ܫܛܢܐ does not occur elsewhere. It is therefore most likely that the translator wrote ܣܛܢܐ = MT which a copyist corrupted to ܫܛܢܐ.

7. בשלם] ܘܫܐܠ ܒܫܠܡ. S. completely misunderstood this name and took it as the noun ܫܠܡ with the preposition ܒ standing pregnantly for ܫܐܠ ܒܫܠܡ = *he saluted.*

מתרדת] ܡܗܪܕܕ. The confusion of ܕ and ܪ and is due to a scribe. Cf. 1 8 where the same error occurs.

8. The section from 4 8–6 18 is in Aramaic.

טעם] ܛܘܓܡܐ which in 4 9, 17, 23 is written ܛܓܡܐ but in each instance appears to be a mistake for ܛܥܡܐ which we must read in all cases. (So also Payne Smith, *Thesaurus Syriacus*, col. 1431). In view of the persistent mistake it may, however, be suggested that ܛܓܡܐ is really τάγμα, although this is ordinarily written ܛܓܡܐ. In 4 18 טעם is translated by ܕܝܛܓܡܐ = διάταγμα.

שמשי] ܫܡܫ]. Without the final yodh occurs also in 4 9, 17, 23.

כנמא] ܐܝܟ ܢܡܘܣܐ. This is a wrong translation which connects נמא with ܢܡܘܣܐ.

9. ואפרסתכיא] ܘܐܦܪܣܝ̈ܐ. The nature of the officials represented by MT is uncertain. S. gives an interpretation. Marquart (cf. notes in Bertholet's "Esra und Nehemia" p. 15) argues for S's reading (ספריא).

טרפליא] ܠܦܣܝ stands for the original ܠܛܦܣܝܐ. A scribe has omitted the ܠ.

ארכוי] ܐܘܚܠ. This shows a confusion of ܣ and ܟ.

דהוא] ܠܘܗܝ, K'rê דהיא.

10. אסנפר] ܐܣܦܡ. This is due to a confusion of ܢ and ܦ and the transposition of the ܣ corrupted to ܦ; originally it was ܐܣܢܦܪ.

בקריה] ܒܩܘܪܝܐ. S. reads "in the cities of (the province of) Samaria". Cf. II. Kings 17 24. This is better than MT. G = S.

ושאר]. S. omits.

וכענת] ܘܐܡܚܕܐ. This transliteration shows that the translator did not understand this word which the Aramaic papyri from Elephantine show was the regular particle (also written כעת and כען) to introduce the matter of a letter after the greeting. It should be translated "to proceed" or "further". Obviously it did not originally occur in this verse; as it stands, it is a copyist's mistake brought in from the following verse (cf. Payne Smith, *Thes. Syr* under ܡܚ col. 1790: "Pro כְּעֶנֶת I. Esd IV. 10, 11 extat in Polygl. ܐܡܚܕܐ, sed codd. Poc. et Uss. in V. 10 exhibent ܐܡܪ ܚܕܐ, in v. 11 ܐܡܚܕܐ. Valet voc. Chald. כְּעֶנֶת sic, ita, et caetera, sed pro nom. prop. habuisse videtur Syrus.") Both MT and S. must be corrected by omitting this word. Cf. Vulg. "in pace"; G. rightly omits.

11. וכענת] ܘܐܡܚܕܐ. Cf. note on vs. 10. Here this word is used correctly.

12. ושורי] ܘܫܘܪܝܗ with suffix = G.

ואשיא] ܘܐܫܝܗ with suffix = G.

13. כען] ܗܫܐ. Cf. note on vs. 10. Again S. misunderstood this word.

מנדה בלו והלך לא ינתנון] ܡܐܠܠ ܠܝ. S. paraphrases MT's "tribute, custom, or toll they will not give" by "there will

38   A CRITICAL EXAMINATION OF THE PESHITTA

be no tribute for thee". This paraphrase omits בלו and הלך which the translator apparently did not understand. בלו is the Assyrian *biltu*; הלך does not occur in Biblical Hebrew. Cf. G.AB. φόροι οὐκ ἔσονται σοι = S. It looks as if S. and G. had read לא להוא לך (cf. Bewer *ad loc.*)

ܘܗܘ ܘܗܝ ܥܠ ܡܠܟܐ] ואפתם מלכים תהנזק. S. again paraphrases MT = "and the royal taxation will suffer damage" by "neither will she (*i.e.* the city) recognize kings" *i.e.* ܐܘ ܗܝ for אפתם which has been a source of conjecture from the earliest time of scientific criticism. The best reading is אפתם. The Greek versions did not know the meaning of this word either. תהנזק is then very freely translated, although S. knew its meaning quite well, cf. vs. 15.

14. כען] ܘܗܫܐ. Cf. note in vss. 10, 11, 13.

ולמלכא]. S. omits.

15. יבקר בספר] ܩܪܝ ܐܢܬ. For MT's "let search be made in the book", S. has "do thou read the book".

ואשתדור] ܘܒܚܘܫܒܢܐ. S. renders freely. Cf. note on 11.

16. ושוריה] ܘܫܘܪܝܗ. S. and G^B follow the K'thib = cf. vs. 12.

חלק] ܫܘܠܛܢܐ. S. renders MT's "part" by "rule". This is a free but good translation.

17. S. connects vss. 16 and 17 by ܘ, the copula.

ושמשי] ܘܫܡܫܝ. S. carries over the force of על.

ואשר] ܘܐܡܪܝܢ ܗܘܘ. This is due to the force of על as above.

כעת] occurs elsewhere as כענת cf. vss. 10, 11. S. reads ܡܢ ܐܡܬܝ and connects with vs. 18. ܡܢ ܐܡܬܝ "when it arrives", represents a mere conjecture on the part of the translator. Cf. vss. 10, 13.

18. עלינא] ܥܠܝ. S. renders correctly and naturally "to me", *i. e.* the king.

קרי] ܩܪܘ. S. renders a passive by 3 pl. active.

19. ובקרו] ܘܒܨܘ. Cf. note on vs. 15.

ואשתדור] ܘܐܣܛܣܝܘܬܐ ܗܘܐ. Cf. vs. 15.

20. ומדה בלו והלך מתיהב להון] ܘܠܡܠܟܐ ܩܕܡܝܐ ܟܠܡܕܡ ܠܐ ܚܫܒܘ ܐܢܘܢ. MT "and tribute, toll, and custom was paid them". S. "and for the former kings they had no regard at all". S. here departs from MT in a radical manner. When we compare this verse with vs. 13, we see that the same difficulty was found with the loan word בלו (biltu) but מנדה was understood, while הלך (not found in Biblical Hebrew) caused difficulty. Here the translator who did not know the correct rendering has done the best he could and paraphrased.

21. כען] ܗܫܐ. Cf. vs. 14.

22. שלו]. S. omits.

מלכין] ܠܡܠܟܐ. Probably the plural sign was carelessly omitted by a copyist.

23. מן־די] ܡܐ ܕܐܬܐ. "When it (the letter) came." This is a free but good translation.

רחום] + ܒܥܠ ܛܥܡܐ. With GL, S. alone preserves the original text. The title בעל־טעם must be inserted in the Aramaic. Cf. vss. 8, 9, 17.

וכנותהון] ܘܩܕܡ ܐܝܠܝܢ ܕܐܟܘܬܗܘܢ. S. renders MT's "their companions" by "and before those who were their equals" as in vs. 7.

אזלו] ܘܪܗܛܘ ܐܙܠܘ. S. renders freely.

באדרע וחיל] ܒܚܝܠܐ ܚܣܝܢܐ.

CHAPTER V

עדוא] ܚܓܝ.

נביאיא] ܢܒܚܐ. S. has quite grammatically "Haggai the prophet and Zechariah the son of Iddo the prophet". This is certainly better than MT and it may present the original text. The alternative is to follow Esd. in omitting נביאה after חגי.

3. שתר בוזני] ܐܫܬܪܒܘܙܢܝ. This is due to a confusion of ܝ and ܐ and to the omission of final ܝ which in the translator's Ms. may not have been written. S. quite correctly writes the names as one word.

להם] ܚܟܝܡܐ ܘܠܗܘܢ. S. freely adds "and to the rest", interpreting MT's "to them" as applying only to the leaders, *i. e.* Zerubbabel and Jeshua.

לשכללה] ܠܫܟܠܠܘ. This is a free but good translation. Cf. 4 16.

4. כנמא] ܢܡܘܣܐ ܐܝܟ. Cf. note on 4 8.

אמרנא] ܐܡܪܘ. S. and G. have preserved here the original text. MT must be emended to read אמרו.

5. אלההם] ܐܠܗܐ. S. and G. omit the suffix.

שבי] ܫܒܝܐ. S. and G. translate "elders of" by "captivity of" because both read שְׁ for שָׂ.

בַּטִּלוּ הִמּוֹ] ܒܛܠܘ. The translator of S. omitted the pronoun and translated the pa'el as pe'al. MT "they did not compel them to stop"; S. "they did not stop".

6. שתר בוזני] ܐܫܬܒܘܙܢ. Cf. note on vs. 3.

אפרסכיא]. S. omits.

7. כלא]. S. omits.

8. לבית]. S. omits.

ואע מתשם בכתליא] ܘܟܦܝܣܐ ܣܓܝܐܐ ܡܬܚܒܪܝܢ ܒܫܘܪܘܗܝ. S. freely renders MT's "and wood is put into the walls" by "and many transverse beams are joined together in its walls".

ועבידתא דך אספרנא מתעבדא ומצלח] ܘܥܒܕܐ ܪܘܪܒܐ ܡܬܥܒܕܝܢ ܬܡܢ. ܘܥܒܕܐ ܪܒܐ ܣܠܩ ܘܐܙܠ ܠܪܝܫܗ. S. paraphrases MT's "and this work is done diligently and prospers" by "and great works are done there; and the great work (literally, goes up. and proceeds to the top) *i. e.* is progressing well". Note אספרנא is translated here by ܪܘܪܒܬܐ, it is omitted in 6 8, but in 6 12 is rendered by ܒܥܓܠ (quickly), in 7 21 it is rendered ܒܚܦܝܛܘܬ (zealously), and in 7 17, 26 by ܒܙܗܝܪܘܬ (carefully).

9. כנמא] ܗܟܢܐ. S. here (also in vs. 11) correctly translates this word. Esd. omits. G^{AB} = MT.

10. שְׁם] ܫܡܗܬܐ. S. and G. here have the plural. But this does not necessitate a different Aramaic original = שמהת.

11. וארעא]. Omits. S. has here the usual form ܐܠܗܐ ܕܫܡܝܐ = אלהי השמים. It is possible that S. has here preserved the better text as the phrase in the Persian period = S.

ובנין ביתא] ܘܒܢܝܢܐ ܕܒܝܬܐ ܗܢܐ ܕܒܢܝܢ. S. is paraphrastic "and the building of this house which we are building".

רב בנהי] ܘܪܘܪܒܢܘܗܝ. S. mistook the two words for one, *i. e.* רַבְרְבָנוֹהִי cf. Dan. 5 1, 3.

12. בבל]. S. omits.

13. בבל] ܕܦܪܣ. S. correctly calls Cyrus King of Persia. MT's connotation is of course original, King of Babylon, is Cyrus's title also in the cuneiform inscriptions. G^{AB} omit. Esd. = βασιλεύοντος Κύρου χώρας Βαβυλωνίας.

14. נבוכדנצר] + ܡܠܟܐ.

להיכלא] ܠܗܝܟܠܗ. Esd. also has the suffix ἐν τῷ ἑαυτοῦ ναῷ.

42   A CRITICAL EXAMINATION OF THE PESHITTA

S's ܠܚܒܠ ܠܗܝܟܠܐ for MT להיכלא די בבל represents a free translation rather than a witness of a different Aramaic original.

ששבצר] ܫܫܒܨܪ. S. has a confusion of ܒ and ܡ.

ויהיבו] ܘܝܗܒ. S. and G. read singular.

15. אחת] ܘܐܚܬ ܣܝܡ. S. freely renders "and bring (and) place".

אלהא]. S. omits.

16. בית אלהא] ܒܝܬܐ. This may not be the original Syriac reading but a scribal corruption of ܒܝܬ ܐܠܗܐ.

17. בבית גנזיא די־מלכא תמה די בבבל] ܒܐ ܚܒܐ ܩܐܠܐ ܕܩܐܠܐ ܘܒܚܒܐ. MT's "in the king's treasury there which is in Babylon", S. renders "in the records, that are in the treasury of the kings of Babylon". That MT here is not the original text Esd. (ἐν τοῖς βασιλικοῖς βιβλιοφυλακίοις τοῦ κυρίου βασιλέως τοῖς ἐν Βαβυλῶνι) as well als S. bear witness. S. presents the nearest to the original (perhaps is original) = בספריא די בבית גנזיא די מלכא די בבל. Cf. Bewer, *ad loc.*

דך] ܕܝ = די. This reading is also in several Aram. Mss. and in Esd. G. has both. S. has the preferable reading.

CHAPTER VI

1. ‎וֹמא‎ ‎חܐܰ‎, ‎אܐ‎ ‎ܗܐ‎ [ובקרו בבית ספריא די גנזיא מהחתין. S. renders MT's "and they searched in the hall of records where the treasures were laid up" by "and he read the records which are in the treasury". S. gives a paraphrastic translation, keeping, as does G., Darius as subject. For the translation of בקר by ‎ܗܡ‎ cf. 4 15, 19.

2. והשתכח] ‎ܘܐܫܬܟܚ‎. S. keeps the same subject as in vs. 1.

באחמתא] ‎ܒܐܚܡܬܐ‎. S. here preserves the original form of the Persian name. Cf. *BDB*.

בבירתא] ‎ܒܪܒܬܐ‎. This may be a corruption of the original ‎ܒܚܣܢܐ‎ which a copyist misread ‎ܒܚܪܒܬܐ‎, as a result of this, מדינתא after בטדי was omitted.

בגוה דכרונה] ‎ܘܗܟܢܐ‎ ‎ܟܬܝܒ‎. MT "(There was written) in it a record". S. "(und thus was written) in the volume". A copyist has inadvertently written ‎ܟܬܒܐ‎ for ‎ܗܟܢܐ‎.

3. שם טעם] ‎ܣܡ‎ ‎ܛܥܡܐ‎ ‎ܘܦܩܕ‎. This is a double translation.

די־בירושלם] ‎ܐܝܟ‎ ‎ܕܐܘܪܫܠܡ‎ = בירושלם. So read several Aram. mss., Esd., G. and Vulg. This is the original text and MT must be corrected accordingly.

ביתא]. S. omits, as do Esd. and G^L, because their construction of the sentence does not require it.

מסובלין] ‎ܢܣܝ‎. This manifestly is a serious scribal mistake for ‎ܢܣܝܒܝܢ‎ = MT.

שתין] ‎ܚܡܫܝܢ‎. S. corresponds here to I. Kings 6 2 and

apparently represents the original. MT was probably occasioned by the proceeding שׁתין.

4. נדבך] ܢܕܒܐ. It is not likely that S. had a different Aramaic text. Either this a free rendering facilitated by the (corrupt) reading חדת which S. follows or it is a scribal correction for the original מִבְחַל.

5. נבוכדנצר] ܡܠܟܐ +. Cf. note on 1 1.

מן־היכלא די־בירושלם]. S. omits through oversight.

ויהתיבון ויהך להיכלא די־בירושלם לאתרה] ܘܐܦ ܐܗܦܟܘ ܘܐܬܘ ܠܐܬܪܗܘܢ ܠܗܝܟܠܐ ܕܒܐܘܪܫܠܡ. S. mistook the sense and translated MT's "let them restore and let it (all) come to the temple which is in Jerusalem, to its place" by "and they restored (them) and they came to their places to the temple which is in Jerusalem". S's suffixes are naturally correct, but that does not mean that S. had a different original Aramaic from MT. ܐܗܦܟܘ and ܠܐܬܪܗ are doublets, of which the latter is secondary. A reader who missed it at the end inserted it.

ותחת] ܘܐܫܠܡܘ. S. translates MT's "and put down" by "and they assembled them together". MT is not correct, but S. translated freely. It seems most likely that the original translator wrote the imperfect of the various verbs in this verse as is demanded by the sense.

6. אפרסכיא] ܐܠܦܐ. S. renders freely.

7. דך פחת יהודיא] ܢܥܒܕܘܢܗ ܝܗܘܕܝܐ. S. translates MT's "that governor of the Jews" by "that the Jews may do it". Some commentators would omit this passage in MT as a gloss. G^B omits, but G^AL follow MT.

שבי] ܫܒܝܐ as in 5 5. S. makes good sense: "Leave the work of the house of God alone that the Jews may do it and also (let alone) the captivity of the Jews that the house of God may be built upon its place." It is not probable, however, that S. had a different underlying Aramaic.

דך]. S. omits.

8. די־תעבדון עם־שבי־יהודיא אלך] ܐܙܕܗܪ ܕܠܐ ܬܬܚܪܘܢ ܥܡ ܫܒܝܬܐ ܕܝܗܘܕܝܐ. S. renders MT's "what you shall do in cooperation with those elders of the Jews", by "take care that you do not quarrel with the captivity of the Jews". S. paraphrases.

אלך]. S. omits.

די מדת] ܘܡܕܐܬܐ. MT "out of the King's revenues which are from the tribute of Abarnahara" allows the Jews to have a portion "of the tribute" while S. more liberally "of the king's revenues and the tribute which (is gotten) in Abarnahara". This is an example of S's free rendering.

אספרנא]. S. omits.

די־לא לבטלא] ܘܡܕܡ ܠܐ ܢܗܘܘܢ ܡܒܛܠܝܢ. S. renders freely.

9. ומה חשחן] ܘܡܕܡ ܕܨܒܝܢ ܗܘܘ ܠܗܘܢ. ܘܡܕܡ ܠܐ ܢܚܣܪܘܢ ܠܗܘܢ S. renders MT's "and what they need" by "and give them what they wish and do not let anything be wanting for them". S. has here not only a doublet, but anticipates also the verb, which it translates again after the catalogue.

כמאמר] ܐܝܟܐ ܕܦܩܕܝܢ. This is a free but good translation.

מתיהב] ܢܗܘܘܢ ܡܝܬܝܢ. S. translates MT's "causing it to be given" by "let them bring (or they shall bring)". This is a free translation.

10. ניחוחין] ܩܘܪܒܢܐ. MT "incense" by "sacrifices" is a free rendering.

לחיי מלכא] ܚܠܦ ܡܠܟܐ. S. freely renders "on behalf of the king" MT's "for the life of the king".

11. וזקיף יתמחא עלהי] ܘܢܥܒܕܘܢ ܠܗ ܙܩܝܦܐ ܘܢܙܩܦܘܢܝܗܝ ܥܠܘܗܝ. MT "and let him be crucified and fastened on it (*i. e.* the beam)". S. "and let them make him a cross and crucify him upon it". S. is a full and free rendering.

12. די שכן] ܕܐܫܟܢ. This is a copyist's error for ܕܐܫܪܝ.

ܐܫܡ]. This is a scribal doublet.

ימגר] ܢܥܡܪ. MT "he shall over throw"; S. "he shall dwell".

S. presents here a scribal error for ܢܣܚܦ. This is a confusion of ܟ and ܦ.

ויתעבד] ܐܡܚܪ. S. "that he quickly perish". A scribe wrote ܐ for ܟ; the original Syr. was ܟܡܚܪ.

13. שתר בוזני] ܐܬܠܢܝܘܣ. This is always so written in Ezra.

לקבל די־] ܡܕܡ ܕ. "Because" is rendered by S. "the thing that".

דריוש מלכא]. S. carelessly omits.

כנמא] ܐܝܟ ܢܡܘܣܐ. S. did not understand this word.

14. שבי] ܫܒܝܬܐ. As in 5 5, 6 7, 8. S. mistakes שׁ for שׂ; in 5 9, however, S. translates correctly.

בנין] ܒܒܢܝܢ. S. translates freely.

עדוא] ܒܪܥܘ. Cf. 5 1.

וארתחששתא] ܘܡܢ ܢܡܘܣܐ ܕܐܪܛܚܫܫܬ. S. repeats the phrase.

16. גלותא] ܫܒܝܐ. S. translates freely.

חנכת בית־אלהא דנה בחדוה] ܥܐܕܐ ܠܒܝܬܐ ܗܢܐ ܕܒܝܬ ܐܠܗܐ ܒܚܕܘܬܐ. MT "the dedication of this house of God with joy"; S. "the feast for this house, which is the house of God, with joy". S. gives a needless repetition.

17. דנה]. S. omits.

לחטיא על־כל־ישראל] ܠܡܫܒܩ ܚܛܗܐ ܕܒܢܝ ܐܝܣܪܝܠ. MT "for a sinoffering for all Israel"; S. "to remit the sins of the Israelites". S. gives a free but good translation.

18. בפלגתהון and במחלקתהון]. S. renders freely by ܒܬܫܡܫܬܗܘܢ.

על־עבידת אלהא] ܥܠ ܥܒܝܕܬܐ ܕܒܝܬܐ ܕܐܠܗܐ. S. agrees with GL and is better than MT. We must insert therefore in the Aramaic text בית before אלהא.

ככתב ספר משה] ܐܝܟ ܕܟܬܝܒ ܒܟܬܒܐ ܕܢܡܘܣܐ ܕܡܘܫܐ. S. renders freely. Cf. note on 1 1.

20. וישחטו הפסח] ܘܢܟܣܘ ܐܢܘܢ ܦܨܚܐ. S. avoids the pregnant

Heb. construction "they killed the passover" by "and they killed the sheep at the passover".

ולהם] ܘܩܛܠ ܠܗܘܢ. S. renders freely.

21. מהגולה] ܡܢ ܓܠܘܬܐ ܕܒܒܠ. S. adds paraphrastically "of Babylon".

וכל] ܘܟܠ. MT has not only the returned exiles but also all others who qualified; S. has only those of the returned who qualified.

אלהא]. S. omits as the sense did not seem to require it.

לדרש] ܡܢ ܠܡܨܠܝܘ. MT "to seek", by S. "to pray before". This is a free rendering.

22. האלהים] ܡܪܝܐ as often in S. cf. 1 6, 8, 3 8, 9.

CHAPTER VII

1. האלה] + ܕܠܘܝ. S. freely expands.

4. עזי] ܥܪܝ. This is a copyist's error for ܥܙܝ. Cf. Neh. 12 19, 42.

5. אלעזר] ܐܠܝܥܙܪ. It is possible that this name was pronounced as by S.

הכהן הראש] ܟܗܢܐ. MT has "Aaron, the high priest". S. takes הראש with the next word, wrongly.

הוא עזרא עלה] ܪܝܫܐ ܗܘܐ ܥܙܪܐ ܕܣܠܩ. MT, "this Ezra went up". S. "Ezra was the first who went up". Cf. vs. 5.

6. מהיר] ܡܗܝܪܐ. S. renders freely.

כיד־יהוה אלהיו עליו כל בקשתו] ܡܘܗܒܬܐ ܐܝܟ ܪܓܬܐ ܢܗܠܟ ܒܢܡܘܣܗ ܕܡܪܝܐ. כל בקשתו is translated by ܡܘܗܒܬܐ ܐܝܟ ܪܓܬܐ. כיד־יהוה אלהיו עליו is represented by ܢܗܠܟ ܒܢܡܘܣܗ ܕܡܪܝܐ. This is strange, for in vs. 9 S. translates this phrase correctly. ܒܢܡܘܣܗ ܕܡܪܝܐ suggests that the translator mistook כיד־יהוה for בדת יהוה and further ܢܗܠܟ suggests that he took the לך of המלך as a verb. S. = "the favor to walk in the law of the Lord as he wished".

7. והמשררים] ܘܡܢ ܡܫܡܫܢܐ. S. omits ו and translates המשרתים v. 15. cf. note on 2 41.

והשערים] ܘܡܢ ܬܪܥܐ. MT "and the porters"; S. "and some of the porters". This is merely a free rendering.

אל ירושלם] + ܘܡܢ ܐܚܪܢܐ ܕܥܡܗܘܢ. S. adds freely.

8. ויבא] ܘܐܬܘ = ויבאו, so also 3 Heb. mss., G^AB and Vulg. MT in Vss. 8—9 considers Ezra as subject and so uses the singular; the versions regard the exiles as subject and so use the plural.

9. באחר]. S. omits.

הוא יסד] ܫܪܝܘ. S. uses pl. as in vs. 8 *q. v.*; but had no different original text.

בא] ܐܬܘ. Cf. note on vs. 8.

כיד־אלהיו הטובה עליו] ܐܝܟ ܐܝܕܐ ܕܐܠܗܐ ܕܡܨܠܚܐ ܠܗܘܢ. MT "According to the good hand of his God upon him". S. "according to the hand of God which prospered them". Both MT and S. consistently carry out their preferences begun in vs. 8.

10. לדרש] ܠܡܥܒܕ. S. renders freely and awkwardly, because the same verb follows almost directly afterwards again. It is therefore a fair question whether the original did not have ܠܡܒܥܐ which is the exact equivalent of לדרש. Cf. 10 16.

חק ומשפט] ܢܡܘܣܐ ܘܕܝܢܐ. The plural signs may of course be due to a copyist.

11. הספר ספר דברי] ܣܦܪ ܕܦܬܓܡܐ. The versions have difficulties with this. G^AB τῷ γραμματεῖ βιβλίου λόγων which corresponds to ספר ספר דברי. Esd. paraphrases 11^b and omits these words. S. simplifies by omitting הספר either deliberately or accidentally.

על־ישראל] ܥܠ ܟܠܗ ܐܝܣܪܝܠ as in 7 1, S. adds ܟܠܗ freely.

12. מלך מלכיא] ܡܠܟܐ ܡܠܟ ܡܠܟܐ. Cf. note on 11.

ספר דתא] ܘܣܦܪܐ ܣܦܪ ܢܡܘܣܐ. S. adds ܘܣܦܪܐ freely.

גמיר] ܫܠܡ. G^AB, Esd., Vulg. have here all incorrectly translated. S. alone has preserved what the epistolatory style demands, viz. "greeting", instead of MT's "perfect". Professor Bewer holds that the present MT is a corruption of what must have stood here, viz: שלם. "Mir scheint in der Tat, in גמיר ein alter Fehler für שלם vorzuliegen, die erste Silbe גמ enthält noch einen Rest davon, die zweite יר scheint mir verdorbene Dittographie des folgenden וכ zu sein. Der ursprüngliche Text lautete also: אלה שמיא שלם. So las auch Pesch."[1]

וכענת]. S. omits. Cf. note on 48.

13. ol ‎ܩܡܝ̱ ܘܦܩܕ ܢܡܘܣܐ [מני שים טעם. S. renders freely and pleonastically to express the formal style.

[לירושלם. S. omits.

14. ol ‎ܩܡܝ̱ ܘܦܩܕ ܢܡܘܣܐ [כל־קבל די מן־קדם מלכא. This is a repetition of vs. 13 where it represents the Aramaic מִנִּי שִׂים טְעֵם.

ܘܫܕܪܘ ܥܡ ‎ܩܡܝܗ̱ܝ. MT "and his seven councillors, thou art sent". S. "and I have sent some of my courtiers". S. does not only put the words in the first person in the mouth of the king, as also in vs. 15, but omits שבעת and misinterprets the meaning of the original. S., of course, gives sense but is in reality nothing but a free and incorrect translation.

ܘܐܦ ܠܡܫܐܠܘ ܥܠ ܢܡܘܣܐ ܕܐܠܗܐ ܕܒܐܝܕܝܟ [בדת אלהך די בידך וכענת, ולבקרא]. MT "according to the law (בדת must be read) of thy God which is in thy hand (i. e. with thee)". S. "and also to inquire about the law of thy God which is in thy hands". If S's text is correctly handed down, the translator repeated for the sake of clearness ܠܡܫܐܠܘ ܥܠ, misunderstanding the meaning of the original. But it is perhaps not quite impossible that this repetition is due to a copyist and that the original translator wrote ܘܠ instead of ܘܐܦ. If he did, his original

---

[1] Bewer: "Der Text des Buches Ezra", S. 69.

read כדת which was the original reading rather than בדת of MT.

ויעטוהי]. S. omits.

15. התנדבו] ܕܐܢܐ ܡܢ ܨܒܝܢܝ ܒܚܘܒܝ ܩܪܒܬ. MT "have freely given". S. "which I have voluntarily offered". This is a free translation put into the first person singular.

לאלה ישראל] ܠܒܝܬܐ ܕܡܪܝܐ. For the interchange in the Divine name cf. 1 5, 3 8, 9, 6 22, 10 1, 6, 9. The addition of ܠܒܝܬܐ is of no consequence for textual purposes.

16. וכל כסף] ܟܠ ܟܣܦܐ. S. omits the copula.

בבל] ܟܠ ܟܠ. ܟܠ is due to dittography.

עם התנדבות עמא] ܥܡܟ ܢܐܙܠ. MT "with the free will offerings of the people". S. "let go with thee". Cf. vs. 13. This is a very poor rendering.

וכהניא]. S. freely adds ܘܟܗܢܐ and understands מתנדבין to refer to the laymen, translating it ܘܐܝܠܝܢ ܕܨܒܝܢ ܠܡܐܙܠ ܥܡܟ "and those who wish to go with thee", and adds ܢܐܙܠܘܢ "let them go", as a result of this faulty interpretation. S. renders very freely and quite incorrectly from an entirely different point of view.

17. בית]. S. omits.

18. כספא ודהבה] ܕܟܣܦܐ ܘܕܗܒܐ. This is due to the influence of vs. 17.

אלהכם] ܐܠܗܟܘܢ. S. translates with Ezra in mind.

19. אלה ירושלם] ܐܠܗܐ ܕܐܘܪܫܠܡ. MT here is quite unparalleled in Ezra. S. presents here the original אלהא די בירושלם, so also Esd., G. and Vulg.

20. ושאר חשחות בית אלהך] ܘܫܪܟܐ ܕܡܐܢܐ ܕܡܬܒܥܝܢ ܠܟ ܠܬܫܡܫܬܐ ܕܒܝܬ ܐܠܗܟ. S. translates very freely.

די יפל לך למנתן]. S. omits.

תנתן] ܬܣܒ ܘܬܬܠ. "Thou shalt take and give." The parallel translation of the entire verse shows the freedom of S.

4*

MT	S.
And whatsoever other requirement of the house of thy God it shall fall to thee to give, thou shalt give it from the king's treasury.	And the rest of the vessels which are required by thee for the service of the house of thy God, thou shalt take, and give from the king's treasury.

21. ספר דתא] ܣܦܪܐ ܣܦܪ ܢܡܘܣܐ. Cf. vs. 11 MT.

יתעבד] ܠܡܥܒܕܘ. S. renders freely.

22. ועד בתין משח] ܥܕܡܐ ܠܡܫܚܐ ܟܘܪܝܢ ܡܐܐ. As in the foregoing in MT and in S. the order should be בתין ועד משח. The order of MT has been confused by a scribe.

23. כל־די] + ܒܟܬܒܐ ܢܬܬܣܝܡ ܘܢܬܝܗܒ ܠܗ. "(Everything) shall be put on a slip of writing", *i. e.*, it shall be carefully noted down for reference, "and give to him", *i. e.*, to Ezra "(according to the precept of the God of heaven.")

יתעבד אדרזדא] ܢܣܒ ܘܢܥܒܕ. MT "let it to be done exactly". S., "he shall take it and use it". S. paraphrases.

24. זמריא תרעיא נתיניא] ܘܩܪܝܢ ܒܩܪܢܬܐ. MT "singers porters, nethinim". S. connects quite wrongly תרעיא with תרועה and got the meaning "trumpeters" for "singers and porters". The *nethinim* S. omitted.

מנדה בלו והלך לא שליט למרמא עליהם] ܠܐ ܫܠܝܛ ܠܡܐܡܪ ܥܠܝܗܘܢ ܡܕܡ. S. omits as previously (cf. 4 13, 20) מנדה בלו והלך and then translates as if its Aramaic original read לא שליט למאמר עליהם. This is in reality merely a careless guess to make a smooth reading and to cover the translator's ignorance of the preceeding words.

25. עזרא] + ܣܦܪܐ. Cf. 1 1.

כחכמת אלהך די בידך] ܐܝܟ ܚܟܡܬܟ ܕܐܠܗܟ ܗܝ ܠܟ.

שפטין] ܕܝܢܐ. S. renders freely.

דתי] ܢܡܘܣܐ. S. translates by a singular. The Greek versions also have the singular which Guthe and others believe is the original reading. Vs. 26 favours the sing. = דָּת.

26. לשרשו] ܣܬܐ. S. paraphrastically renders by the word that makes the natural antithesis to "death".

27. כזאת] ܡܐܟܠܐ ܗܕܐ. This is a free but good translation.

אשר]. S. omits.

28. ויועציו ולכל]. S. omits.

ܐܝܕܐ ܕܐܠܗܐ ܗܘܬ ܥܠܘܗܝ ܡܛܠ [כיד יהוה. S. paraphrases.

CHAPTER VIII

ܘܗܠܝܢ ܫܡܗܬܐ ܕܪ̈ܝܫܐ. [ואלה ראשי]. S. adds freely after (and these are) "the names of" because a list of names follows.

ܐܚܒ̈ܬܟܘܢ [אבתיהם]. A scribe has carelessly changed the pronominal ending.

[והתיחשם] ܘܐܬܚܫܒܘ. S. renders MT's "and their genealogy" by "who were reckoned by genealogy." This is a free translation. The following comparison of MT and S. shows the freedom the translator used:

MT	S.
Now these are the chiefs of their fathers and their genealogy, (viz.) the ones going up with me in the reign of Artaxerxes, the king, from Babylon.	Now these are *the names of the* chiefs of *your* fathers *who were reckoned by genealogy* and went up with me, in the reign of Artaxerxes, the king, from Babylon.

2. [איתמר] ܐܝܬܡܪ for the original ܐܝܬܡܪ. A scribe has written the shorter form as a result of haplography due to the similar ending of the preceding word.

3. [מבני] ܡܢ ܒܢܝ.

4. [פחת מואב] ܦܚܬ ܡܘܐܒ. S's usual way of writing this. Cf. note on 2 6.

[אליהועיני בן] ܐܠܝܐ ܘܥܢܢܝ ܒܪ ܙܟܪܝܐ. S. wrongly divides this name into two names אליה וענני which necessitates the changing of ܒܢ into ܒܪ.

5. בן־יחזיאל] ܥܕܘ ܒܪ ܢܚܙܐܝܠ. S. has just as Esd.AB and GA Ζαθοής = זַתּוּא which has dropped from MT, for ܥܕܘ was certainly ܙܬܘ. Esd.AB and GA insert זַתּוּא after מבני, S. after שכניא. ܢܚܙܐܝܠ is a scribal corruption of ܝܚܝܐܝܠ.

6. ומבני] ܡܢ ܒܢܝ without the copula.

עדין] ܥܘܐܝܢ. Cf. note on 74 for a similar scribal error. The original ܥܘܕܝܢ or rather ܥܕܝܢ has easily been changed because of the similarity of ܐ and ܕ. The ע here has the hard sound = ܥ as in Gomorrah = עמרה. S. follows a different vocalization than that of the Massorites.

עבד] ܥܒܕܘ. ܘ was perhaps originally the copula with the next word; in any case it is wrong.

7. עתליה] ܢܛܠܝܐ. S. presents again a scribe's confusion of ܥ with ܢ, and of ܬ with ܛ for the original ܥܬܠܝܐ.

8. זבדיה] ܙܪܒܝܐ. S. presents here a scribal confusion of ܪ and ܕ and ܒ and ܒ.

9. ויחיאל] ܢܚܝܐܝܠ. S. presents the easy confusion of ܢ for ܝ. The original of course was ܝܚܝܐܝܠ. Cf. vs. 5.

10. שלומית בן־יוספיה] ܫܠܡܘܬ. ܫܠܡܘܬ. ܒܪ ܢܘܣܦܝܐ. The MT has evidently lost a word. S. noticed this and supplied it by writing ܫܠܡܘܬ twice, in this way trying to make sense. We know from GA and Esdras that the missing word was βαανι = בָּנִי which MT lost by haplography. ܢܘܣܦܝܐ is due to confusion of ܢ and ܝ and different vocalization. MT should read ומבני בָּנִי שלומית etc.

מאה] ܡܐܬܝܢ so also Esd.syr.

11. בבי] ܒܟܝ. S. so in each case (twice), Esd.L GL have βοκχεί = S.

12. עזגד] ܥܙܓܕ for original ܥܙܓܪ; confusion of ܕ and ܪ.

הקטן] ܙܩܘܪܐ is a copyist's error for ܙܥܘܪܐ. A scribe has confused ܩ and ܥ.

עשרה] ܚܡܫܐ. This reading is also found in 38 Heb. Mss. and in Esd. L.

13. אדניקם] ܐܕܘܢܩܡ for original ܐܕܢܝܩܡ. Confusion of ܘ and ܝ and of ܢ and ܡ.

יעואל] ܢܚܠܐ for original ܝܚܠܐ. Confusion of ܢ and ܝ.

14. וזבוד] ܘܙܒܕ. S. follows the K'rê of the Hebrew text, וְזַכּוּר Vulg., Esd. LB also read as S. This is the original.

ועמו] ܘܚܒܪܘܗܝ so also several Heb. Mss.

שבעים] ܫܒܥܝܢ. This is a mistake due to the preceding verse.

15. נחנה] ܗܘܝܢ. This is a free translation.

אהוא] ܗܘܐ. So also vss. 21, 31.

לאליעזר] ܠܐܠܝܥܙܪ, originally this was ܠܐܠܝܥܙܪ, so Thorndyke.

16. אלנתן] ܐܠܢܬܢ for original ܐܠܢܬܢ.

לריב] ܠܪܒܐ. for original ܠܪܝܒܐ.

ויריב] ܘܪܝܒܐ for original ܘܪܝܒܐ.

מבינים] ܗܢܘܢ ܟܠܗܘܢ ܪܝܫܐ. S., as the text stands, paraphrases by "these were all of them chiefs" but the ܪܝܫܐ is a mistake due to the preceding ܪܝܫܐ. Originally the text read ܡܒܝܢܐ or ܡܒܝܢܝܢ which is the exact equivalent of מבינים.

למשלם] ܠܡܫܠܡ. This is the usual Syriac vocalization in Ezra.

17. ואוצאה] ܘܦܩܕܬ = Ḳ're of MT = וָאֲצַוֶּה. This is preferable to the K'thib.

אדו] ܐܕܪܝ. The mater lectionis was lacking in the translator's MS.

הראש] ܪܝܫܐ ܕܟܗܢܐ. S. translates freely.

אדו] ܐܕܪܝ mistake for ܐܕܘ as before.

אחיו] ܐܚܘܗܝ, a correction of the translator.

הנתינים] ܗܢܘܢ ܕܥܡܪܘ. S. renders MT's "Nethinim" by "those who dwelt", misunderstanding it and connecting it with the late Heb. meaning of נתן.

18. הטובה] ܛܒܬܐ. Cf. note on 7 9.

ושרביה] ܘܫܪܒܝܐ. A copyist has omitted the ܪ in ܫܪܒܝܐ.

שמנה עשר [ܬܡܢܥܣܪ̈ܐ]. S. has 12 for MT's 18. This is a copyist's error. S. usually agrees with MT in numbers much closer than does Esd. but cf. note on vs. 26 below.

20. נתינים (twice). S. translates by ܥܒ̈ܕܐ and by ܢܬܝܢ̈ܐ. S. felt the original force of the word. We are used to regard Nethinim almost like a name; but it was merely the designation of the old temple slaves.

והשרים] S. omits through oversight.

בשמות [ܒܫܡܗܬܗܘܢ]. S. renders freely.

21. שם צום [ܨܡܢ ܗܟܝܠ]. The translator misunderstood צום "fast", and connected it with צוה "command". ם he took as the suffix, and ש he omitted.

ישרה] ܠܡܪܝܐ was probably ܡܪܝܐ originally.

לטפנו [ܠܛܠܝܢ]. The Syriac reading is here probably corrupt. The original read ܠܛܦܠܢ or ܠܛܦܠܐ.

22. על] ܥܡ. S. renders freely MT's "upon" by "with".

מאויב [ܒܥܠܕܒܒ̈ܐ]. S. translates a collective by a plural. Cf. vs. 31.

אלהינו [ܐܠܗܐ]. S. omits the suffix here but in vs. 23 = MT. This may perhaps be a scribal corruption from ܐܠܗܢ as vs. 23.

24. שרי] ܪܘܪ̈ܒܢܐ is regarded by the translator as an equivalent, — a free rendering. Cf. 9 2.

חשביה [ܘܚܫܒܝܐ]. S. with Esd. AB preserves an original reading. Cf. Bewer ad loc.

25. ואשקולה [ܡܢܝܬ]. S. freely renders MT's "weighed" by "counted".

תרומת [ܐܪܡܬ]. S. renders freely.

וייעצו [ܘܡܠܟܘܗܝ], a free translation.

הנמצאים] + ܠܗ freely.

26. על-ידם] S. renders freely by ܠܗܘܢ.

שש-מאות וחמשים [ܓܕܐ ܘܣܒܥܝܢ]. This is an unusual case because S. agrees with MT regarding numerals much better than the other versions.

וכלי־כסף מאה לככרים זהב מאה ככר] S. (as Esd. A) omits.

27. לאדרכנים] ܘ,ܢܡܚܐ. S. translates ל by ܘ.

כפרי] ܡܓ̈ܠܐ. S. freely renders "bowls" by "platters."

מצהב] ܡܥܠܝܐ. S. translates freely "corinthian" which is a synonym for precious. Cf. I. Kings 7 45. I. Ch. 29 7.

שנים] S. omits.

חמודת] ܪܓܝܓܝ. S. renders quite freely.

29. תשקלו] ܬܠܡܚܘܢ. Cf. vss. 25, 26, 33.

הלשכות] ܓܙܐ. S. renders freely.

30. S. adds ܟܠܗܘܢ.

משקל] ܒܡܢܝܢܐ ܕܡܠܐ. S. renders freely.

31. אויב] ܕܒܒܝܗܘܢ. S. translates a collective by a plural, as in vs. 22.

33. על־יד] ܥܠ ܐܝܕܝ. S. translates freely.

ויובד] ܢܚܘܪ. This is a scribe's error for ܢܥܒܕ.

נועדיה] ܥܘܕܝܐ for original ܥܘܝܕܐ. A scribe has miscopied.

בנוי] ܒܢܝ. The translator mistook בנוי for בני.

34. במשקל] ܒܡܢܝܢܐ. The copula must be inserted in MT, as Esd., G., Vulg., as well as S. show.

35. בני] ܒܢܝ. S. renders freely.

צפירי חטאת] ܨܦܪܝܐ ܚܠܦ ܚܛܗܐ. Cf. 6 17.

הכל עלה] ܟܠܗܘܢ ܣܠܩܘ. S. translates freely but well; the original Heb. did of course not read עלות.

36. דתי] ܦܘܩܕܢܐ = διάταγμα, G^AB τὸ νόμισμα. S. knows of only one decree.

נשאו] ܘܗܘܘ ܡܝܩܪܝܢ. S. translates MT's "helped" by "were honoring". The translator misunderstood the meaning (cf. 1 4) employed here by MT thinking it signified "lift up" = honor. Esd. and G made the same error.

CHAPTER IX

1. אלה] + ܒܠܚܘܕ.

השרים] ܩܫܝ̈ܫܐ. S. translates here according to the sense.

העם ישראל] ܥܡܐ ܕܐܝܣܪܝܠ. S. translates as if MT read עם ישראל but S. had no different original text.

הארצות] ܡܕܝܢ̈ܬܐ. This is the usual translation in Ezra. Cf. 3 3, 9 2, 7.

כתעבתיהם] ܒܛܢ̈ܦܘܬܗܘܢ = בתעבתיהם so also G, and this was most probably the original reading.

הפרזי היבוסי העמני המאבי המצרי]. S. has different order, ܘܟܢܥܢܝ̈ܐ ܘܦܪ̈ܙܝܐ ܘܥܡܘܢܝ̈ܐ ܘܡܨܪ̈ܝܐ ܘܡܘܐܒܝ̈ܐ.

2. השרים והסגנים] ܕܩܫܝ̈ܫܐ ܘܕܟܗ̈ܢܐ. The translator here disagrees with MT which holds the political officials guilty. The translator of S. holds the religious leaders guilty. This is of course only an interpretation by S., who had the same text as MT. G omits והסגנים which leads Guthe, Bertholet and others to hold it to be a doublet of שרים. Bewer, on the other hand, upholds the MT. Cf. *"Der Text des Buches Ezra"* ad loc.

3. בגדי] ܢܚ̈ܬܝ. S. with Esd. and G. reads the plural בְּגָדַי which is to be preferred to MT.

4. כל חרד בדברי] ܟܠ ܐܝܠܝܢ ܕܚܫܝܚܝܢ ܗܘܘ ܥܠܝܗܘܢ ܥܠ ܡܠܬܐ. S. "all who were concerned about the word" (sing.) The singular ܥܠ ܡܠܬܐ = בדבר was probably the original reading. It is vouched for also by Esdras and Vulg.

60 A CRITICAL EXAMINATION OF THE PESHITTA

הגולה] ܡܚܒܠ ܚܒܠ ܐܚܠܡܗ,ܘ. S. renders freely but well.

למנחת הערב] ܒܚܫܐܐܐܐ. S. renders paraphrastically, substituting the time "ninth hour" for the "evening offering" which was at this time (3 p. m.) Cf. Acts 3 1.

5. במנחת הערב] ܚܒܪܠ, ܘܠܩܕ ܗܥܝ. Cf. note on vs. 4.

בקרעי] ܥܡ ܨܘܝܕ. S. renders freely.

בגדי] ܡܢܐܠ plur. as in vs. 3, also here correct.

ואפרשה כפי] S. adds freely ܚܪܠܐܐ the correct explanation.

אל] ܗܥܡ. S. shows a fine sense of reverence.

אלהי] ܐܠܗܐ. S. omits the suffix.

6. בשתי ונכלמתי] ܚܒܗܠܝ. S. reads plural; MT sing.

אלהי] ܐܠܗܝ. S. reads plural and changes order of words.

פני] ܐܩܝ plur. suffix.

ואשמתנו גדלה] ܗܬܠܗܥܝ ܘܐܘܚܠ plur. S. freely adds ܣܠܚܗ.

7. אנחנו] S. adds freely but well ܐܗܚܣܝ.

באשמה גדלה] S. plur. as in vs. 6.

ובעונתינו נתנו] ܡܠܐܐ ܘܐܨܗܝ .... ܡܗܠܚܗܐ ܐܚܠܗܝ. S. paraphrases.

בשבי ובבזה]. S. has the reverse order.

ואנחנו] S. adds freely ܘܐܚܢܝ.

ביד מלכי הארצות] S. adds freely ܘܚܠܟܝܚܚܝ, ܘܚܠܒܠ. S. changes the order and paraphrases freely in this verse.

8. כמעט רגע] ܚܡ ܡܠܠܐ. ܪܚܘܝ. This is free and good.

יהוה]. S. omits, as does G[B].

יתד] ܘܘܡܐܠ,. S. translates freely.

ולתתנו]. S. omits suffix.

9. ויט עלינו]. S. adds ܐܠܗܢ.

מחיה] ܡܘܢܣܥܝ ܘܥܐܐܠ. S. translates freely by "our daily support".

לרומם] ܘܢܪܡܝܥ freely.

לתת־לנו] ܘܢܐܠܐ ܠܢ freely.

10. נאמר]. S. adds freely ܡܪܗܥܝ.

זאת] ܘܐܠܝ ܡܠܗܥܝ. S. renders freely, cf. 9 1.

11. צוית]. S. adds suffix freely ܦܩܕܬ.

ארץ]. S. omits as unnecessary in the translation.

לאמר] ܘܐܡܪܬ ܠܢ. S. renders freely.

עמי הארצות] ܕܥܡܡ̈ܐ ܘܕܐܪ̈ܥܬܐ, probably the copula is due to a copyist.

בטמאתם] ܘܒܛܢܦܘܬܗܘܢ. ܡܛܠ ܗܢܐ. S. paraphrases.

12. והורשתם] ܘܬܐܪܬܘܢ ܘܬܫܒܩܘܢ. S. translates pleonastically and not very differently from MT = "and leave it for an inheritance".

13. כל] ܘܥܠ ܟܠܗܝܢ. Cf. vs. 1, 10.

באשמתנו הגדלה] ܘܒܚܛܗ̈ܝܢ ܪ̈ܘܪܒܐ plur. as in vs. 7.

חשכת למטה מעונינו] ܐܬܚܫܒܬ ܥܠܝܢ ܠܡܫܒܩ ܚܛܗ̈ܝܢ. MT "thou hast punished us less than our sins (warrant)". S. "thou hast planned for us to forgive our sins". This comes from the reading חשבת for חשכת which 9 Heb. Mss. have.

כזאת] ܟܕܟܠܗܝܢ. S. renders freely.

14. הנשוב להפר] ܣܛܝܢ ܐܬܦܢܝܢ ܘܥܒܪܢ. S. loses the rhetorical question of MT rendering, "Is it possible that again we shall trespass" by "We have turned away and trespassed". G makes a similar error.

ולהתחתן] ܘܐܙܠܢ ܘܕܒܩܢ. Again S. overlooks the question MT "or marry people of these abominations" and renders freely "and we went and clung to these unclean folks"; and freely adds ܘܥܒܪܢ ܐܝܟ ܥܒܕܝܗܘܢ. S. disregards the question again and presents here a lengthy paraphrase: "But thou art merciful. Thou wilt not be angry with us. Forgive our transgressions from before thee. Because thou art merciful, leave us remnants in the world, because there is none like thee ; and may we not perish."

15. הננו לפניך באשמתנו] ܚܢܢ ܩܝܡܝܢ ܘܡܘܕܝܢ ܩܕܡܝܟ ܥܠ ܚܛܗ̈ܝܢ. S. paraphrases: "We stand and confess before thee our sins."

לעמוד] ܠܡܩܡ ܩܕܡܝܟ ܘܠܐ. S. paraphrases.

CHAPTER X

1. בכה ומתנפל] ܢܗܘܐ ܒܟܐ ܘܐܡܪ. S. changes the word order.
האלהים] ܡܪܝܐ. Cf. 1 5, 3 8, 9, 6 22, 7 15.

בכו העם] ܒܟܘ ܥܡܐ. S. renders instead of "the people wept"; "the children were weeping".

הרבה בכה] ܒܟܐ ܐܚܕ ܠܗ. Cf. 1 1.

2. יחיאל] ܝܚܝܐܠ is a scribal confusion of ܐ for ܠ. The original was ܝܚܝܠ.

עולם] ܥܠܡ = MT K're עֵילָם.

+ [לעזרא] ܥܙܪܐ. Cf. note on 1 1.

באלהינו] ܐܠܗܢ ܕܝܠܢ. Cf. vs. 1.

3. נכרת־ברית לאלהינו] ܠܢ ܡܘܡܬܐ ܩܕܡ ܐܠܗܢ. S. translates freely MT's "let us make a covenant with our God" by "let us say oaths before our God".

נשים] ܢܫܐ ܢܘܟܪܝܬܐ. MT is obviously incorrect as only the foreign wives were meant. G^ABL support the reading of S., accordingly we should emend MT to read הַנָּכְרִיּוֹת נָשִׁים. It is possible that the translator has used his prerogative of making clear what was meant and that the original text read הנשים or נשינו. Professor Bewer (ad loc) adopts the latter on the ground that "Die Einfügung lässt sich leicht, die Auslassung schwer erklären".

בעצת] ܒܡܠܟܐ ܕܝܠܗ = כעצת. So also G^AB and many oriental Heb. mss. This is the correct reading; the interchange of

ב and כ was easily made in the Heb. MT must be accordingly mended.

וַיֵּעָשֵׂה] ܚܟܡ. MT "let it he done". S. "do". S. connects the following קוּם cf. vs. 4 with this imperative ܘܐܠܡ "and confirm". MT is better.

4. עֲלָיִךְ הַדָּבָר] ܘܐ ܦܣܩܐ ܗܘ ܚܠܦܝܟ. S. paraphrases "(for) on thy account this decision has been decided".

וַאֲנַחְנוּ] ܣܘܥܠܐ ܘܣܝ. ܣܘܥܠܐ ܘ is repeated because of the foregoing paraphrase.

עֶזְרָא] + ܣܦܪܐ. Cf. note on I 1, 10 2.

5. שָׂרִי] ܡܩܬܡܐ. This is S's usual paraphrase of this word. Cf. 8 24, 9 1.

הַכֹּהֲנִים הַלְוִיִּם] ܣܘܡܣܐ ܘܠܘܝܐ. S. reads the copula with G^ABL and Esd. This is obviously the original reading = הכהנים והלוים.

כַּדָּבָר] ܦܣܩܐ ܝܗܒ. S. brings out the specific sense of כדבר here.

6. עֶזְרָא] + ܣܦܪܐ. As in vss. 2 and 5.

הָאֱלֹהִים] ܐܠܗܝ. As in vs. 1.

לִשְׁכַּת] ܐܣܟܦܐ. S. reads pl.

אֶלְיָשִׁיב] ܐܠܣܒ. S. is the result of scribal carelessness which changed ܐܠܝܣܒ into ܐܠܣܒ by miscopying the ܒ. Esd. AB and G^AB vouch for the originality of MT.

וַיֵּלֶךְ] ܘܐܙܠ = וַיֵּלֶן. A scribe has carelessly written ךְ for ן in MT. S. preserved the original reading. Cf. Esd.

הַגּוֹלָה] ܓܠܘܬܐ. S. paraphrases.

7. וַיַּעֲבִירוּ קוֹל] ܘܐܟܪܙܘ ܟܗܢܐ. S. freely and correctly paraphrases MT's "they made proclamations" by "and the priests proclaimed".

יְרוּשָׁלַם] ܒܐܘܪܫܠܡ. S. here has preserved the original which is vouched for by many Heb. Mss. also by G. The context also demands it in agreement with the previous "in Judea".

לכל] ܘܒܟܠ. Again S. construes as in the foregoing and reads "and among all the captives." In MT the proclamation is to the exiles alone; S. has it to all the province of Judea, to the capital *and* to the exiles.

ירושלם] + ܡܕܝܢܬܐ. Cf. note on 1 1.

8. כעצת] + ܢܗܘܐ ܠܗ. S. renders freely.

השרים והזקנים] ܕܩܫܝ̈ܫܐ ܘܕܪ̈ܘܪܒܢܐ. S. has a different order.

מקהל הגולה] ܡܢ ܟܢܫܐ ܕܫܒܝܬܐ. S. interprets. Cf. vs. 6.

9. הוא חדש] ܕܬܫܥܐ. S. renders freely.

בעשרים] ܒܥܣܪܬܐ. This is due to a scribe's carelessness.

ישבו] ܩܡܘ. S. renders freely.

ברחוב בית]. S. omits through oversight.

האלהים] ܕܡܪܝܐ. Cf. vs. 1.

מרעידים על־הדבר ומהגשמים] ܘܙܝܥܝܢ ܘܪܬܝܬܝܢ ܥܠ ܡܠܬܐ. "Quaking and shivering because of the matter." S. either translated pleonastically מרעידים (cf. vs. 12) and omits ומהגשמים (cf. vs. 12) or took the latter wrongly for ומנעשים.

10. מעלתם] + ܠܟܠܗܘܢ. Cf. vs. 2.

אשמת] ܕܣܟܠܘ̈ܬܐ. S. reads plur. as usual.

12. קהל] ܟܢܫܐ. S. interprets as in vss. 6 and 8.

ויאמרו] + ܟܠܗܘܢ. Cf. note on 1 1.

כן כדבריך עלינו לעשות]. If S. is not simply a free paraphrase, its present text may contain a doublet of which the original ܫܡܥܝܢ ܦܬܓܡܝܟ ܠܘܬܢ "thy words to us" was *later* corrected by ܘܡܩܒܠ ܟܠܡܕܡ ܕܐܡܪܬ ܠܢ ܠܡܥܒܕ ܒܩܘܫܬܐ "and acceptable is everything which thou tellest us to do in truth". Perhaps the second translation (correction) was written on the margin and a later scribe incorporated it into the text. We may still further ask, was ܒܩܘܫܬܐ still another translation of כן?

13. אבל] ܒܪܡ ܕܝܢ. S. translates freely.

אין כח] + ܠܢ. S. translates freely.

14. לכל־הקהל] ܘܟܠܗ ܟܢܫܐ. S. did not represent the meaning

of the original correctly according to which the leaders were to represent the whole congregation in this matter. On ܟܢܫܐ cf. vs. 12.

לעתים מזמנים] ܠܥܕܢܐ ܕܨܠܘܬܐ. S. here misinterprets "the appointed times" by "the time of prayer".

חרון אף] ܚܡܬܗ. S. uses one term for the two Hebrew words.

עד לדבר הזה] ܡܛܠ ܡܣܥܪܢܘܬܐ ܗܕܐ. MT is evidently wrong and must be corrected here to על הדבר הזה. Two Heb. Mss. GAB Vulg. read על. It is true that S. paraphrases in ܡܣܥܪܢܘܬܐ but has the exact sense, and may therefore be regarded as a witness of the true text.

15. עשהאל] ܥܣܗܐܝܠ. This is a copyist's carelessness for the original ܥܣܐܝܠ. Cf. v. 6 for a similar mistake in the Syriac.

יחזיה] ܚܘܝܐ. This is a scribal error for ܚܙܝܐ.

ܘܡܫܠܡ]. A copyist has misplaced this name.

על־זאת] ܥܠ ܡܠܬܐ ܗܕܐ = על הדבר הזה. Cf. note on 11.

שבתי] ܡܬܝ. This is a confusion of ש (written here ܫ) and ܡ (cf. first word in this verse where a similar error occurs and also vs. 6) with the omission of ܒ.

עֲזָרָם] ܥܕܪܗܘܢ. S. points the Heb. differently and renders here "(was) their helper", the subject is Shabbethai, the Levite. In MT Meshullam, who is misplaced in S., was also the subject, "they helped them".

16. ויבדלו] ܘܦܪܫ. S. with GL καὶ διέστειλεν gives evidence of an original וַיַּבְדֵּל which MT also demands in that Ezra alone is subject. MT must here be corrected.

אנשים] + ܒܚܝܪܐ. S. freely adds ܒܚܝܪܐ.

בשמות] + ܐܬܩܪܝ. S. has a free addition to bring out the meaning.

לְדַרְיוֹשׁ] ܠܡܬܒܥܘ ܥܠ = לְדרוש, This is the correct reading. MT must accordingly be corrected.

17. בכל האנשים] ܡܠܬܝ̈ ܚܒܪ̈ܝ = בכל אנשים. This is the correct reading. MT must be accordingly corrected.

18. ויריב] ܣܥܒܪ. The translator read the fuller from ויריב = ܣܥܒܪ which a scribe corrupted into ܣܥܒܕ.

19. ויתנו ידם] ܘܐܫܬܥܒܕܘ ܐܦ ܗܢܘܢ. S. renders freely "and they also consented".

ואשמים] ܩܪܒܘ. S. omits ואשמים and supplies "they offered" in order to make sense. Cf. RV. which reads both.

איל־צאן] ܐܡܪ̈ܐ, ܕܥܢܐ. S. has the plural.

20. אמר] ܐܡܠ. Cf. 2 59.

זבדיה] ܙܒܕܘ. S. reads with 9 Hebrew Mss. that which may have been the original. The confusion is as easily explained in Hebrew as in Syriac.

21. יחיאל] ܚܢܢܝܐܠ. This is a scribal corruption of the original ܝܚܝܐܠ.

22. אליועיני] ܐܠܝ. In vs. 27, S. has ܐܠܝܘܥܝܢܝ which shows that the original was ܐܠܝܘܥܝܢܝ in vs. 27 and ܐܠܝܥܢܝ here.

ישמעאל] ܣܡܥܐܠ. This is an error for ܐܝܫܡܥܐܠ.

נתנאל] ܢܬܢܐܠ. S. gives here the other common form of this name.

יוזבד] ܣܘܪܒܕ. This is due to an exchange of ܪ and ܘ for the original ܝܘܙܒܕ.

23. יוזבר] ܣܘܪܒܕ. This is due to a scribe's carelessly writing ܒ for ܕ and ܘ for ܝ.

ומדמנה הוא קלימא] ܡܕܠܐ ܘܩܠܝܐ. S. interprets the names as belonging to two distinct individuals; but this is due to the carelessness of a scribe who wrote ܘ for ܗܘ. ܡܕܠܐ shows the confusion of ܝ for ܢ.

24. המשרתים] ܡܫܡܫܢܐ = המשרתים. Cf. 2 41.

אלישיב] ܐܠܫܒ. This is the result of careless copying. The original was ܐܠܝܫܒ. A scribe changed ܝ and ܒ to ܢ. Cf. the same error in vs. 6.

שלם] ܫܠܡܘ. This is due to the absence of *mater lectionis* in MT; the final ܘ is a dittography of the following copula.

אורי] ܐܘܕܝ. This is due to an interchange of ܪ and ܕ for the original ܐܘܪܝ.

25. יזיה] ܝܙܝܐ. The ܢ is dittography for ܝ.

מימן] ܒܢܝܡܝܢ. A careless scribe has written a more common name which resembled closely the one he found in his text.

אלעזר] ܠܥܙܪ. This is for the original ܐܠܝܥܙܪ or ܐܠܥܙܪ.

26. מתניה] ܡܬܢܝܐ. The aural confusion here is due to both names being so common and thus easy to confuse.

יחיאל] ܢܢܝܐܝܠ. This is a corruption of the original ܝܚܝܐܝܠ or ܝܚܐܝܠ by a confusion of ܢ and ܝ and of ܢ and ܚ.

אליה] ܐܠܝܗܘ. This form is due to the following copula which S. connects with the fuller form of the name אליהו.

27. זתוא] ܙܝ̈ܬܐ. The seiāme points are, of course, a scribal error, due, perhaps, to a thoughtless connection with "olive trees". The mistaken pronunciation again may come from the name זֵיתָא = ܙܝܬܐ.

אליועני] ܐܠܝܥܢܝ. This is for the original ܐܠܝܘܥܝܢܝ. Cf. note on vs. 22 also 8 4.

אלישיב] ܐܠܝܫܒ. *Mater lectionis* was wanting in Ms. used by translator.

מתניה] ܡܬܢܝܐ. Cf. vs. 26.

זבד] ܙܒܪ. This is due to an interchange of ܕ and ܪ and to a different vocalization.

עזיזא] ܥܙܝܐ. This is a copyist's corruption of the original ܥܙܝܙܐ due to the more common but different name.

29. בני] ܒܒܝ. S. reads as does one Heb. Ms. Confusion of ܢ and ܒ.

משלם] ܡܢ ܐܠܗܘܡ. This may be due to a careless copyist rather than to the translator.

עדיה] ܚܕܝܐ. S. reads as does one Heb. Ms. Confusion of ו and י. Cf. v. 28.

וישוב] ܝܫܘܒ. This is a scribe's careless copying.

שאל] ܫܐܘܠ. S. supplied the more common pronunciation.

30. פחת] ܡܥܓܠ. S. always so translates in Ezra.

עדנא] ܥܓܢܐ. The ܠ is a mistake ܐ and the ܢ is a mistake for ܒ. Note how a good common name results from these mistakes.

ובנוי ומנשה [ובנוי מנשה] ܘܚܕܝܘܗܝ ܚܒܪ ܡܢܫܐ = ובני מנשה. The translator missed the word and by the interchange of י and ו has changed the name "Binnui" into "his sons".

31. ובני חרם] ܥܡ ܚܒܪ ܣܥܡ. S. and G^{AB} also many Heb. Mss. have here the original reading. MT must be corrected to read וּמִבְּנֵי. G^{AB} Esd. ABL all vocalize חָרָם as S. does. MT = חָרִם which must also be corrected to חָרָם.

ישיה מלכיה] ܡܠܟܝܐ ܐܝܫܐ. S. has here a different order. S. read originally ܐܘܫܐ for ܐܝܫܐ.

32. שמריה] ܣܡܪܢܐ. A copyist mistook this for the more common name.

33. מתתה] ܡܐܐܠ. S. vocalizes differently.

זבד] ܙܡܝ. S. again confuses ו and י and ܒ and ܡ.

ירמי] ܝܪܡܝܐ. This is a copyist's error for ܝܪܡܝ. A scribe has confused ܕ and ܒ and ܪ and ܝ.

34. בני] ܚܒܝ. Cf. vs. 29 where the "sons of Bani" are already listed. S. must be correct as one clan would not be listed twice. At least one is wrong either in vs. 29 or here. MT should therefore probably be corrected to S. = בכי.

מעדי] ܡܥܕܝ. This is due to a different vocalization.

אואל] ܝܘܐܠ = יוֹאֵל to which Esd. ABL and G^{BL} also testify. Cf. Bewer ad loc. MT must be accordingly corrected.

35. בדיה] ܒܝ. A copyist read ו for י and this led to the omission of יה, hence ܒܝ.

כלוהי, Ḳ're כלוהו] ܟܠܝܗܘ = כליהו which may have preserved the original reading.

36. וניה] ܘܢܘܐܝܠ. MT is corrupt; but S. does not seem to have preserved the correct reading.

אלישיב] ܐܠܝܫܒ. Cf. vs. 27.

37. ויעשו, Ḳ're ויעשי] ܥܡܠܘ. S. in its corrupted state seems to have followed Ḳ're and to have read originally ܥܡܫ. (Cf. note on vs. 36). ܫ was corrupted to ܠܘ.

38. ובני ובנוי] ܘܒܢܝ ܒܢܘܝ. This is a scribal corruption for the original ܘܒܢܝ ܒܢܘܝ, i. e., the second without ܘ = "and the sons of Binnui," so also G. MT must be accordingly corrected.

39. עדיה] ܥܙܪܐ. Cf. vs. 29. A scribe mistook it for the common name, an aural error. ד softly and badly spoken sounded like ז. Cf. Heb. עזר and Syr. ܥܕܪ and the French pronunciation of the English *th*.

40. מכנדבי] ܡܟܡܕܝ. This is for ܡܟܢܕܒܝ. But both MT and S. are corrupt.

שרי] ܣܪܝ. The translator read שׂ for שׁ.

41. עזראל] ܥܕܪܐܝܠ. This is a corruption for the original ܥܙܪܐܝܠ in its Syriac form.

ושלמיהו]. S. omits.

43. יעיאל] ܢܥܘܐܝܠ. This is a copyist's mistake for the original ܝܥܘܐܝܠ.

מתתיה] ܘܡܬܬܝܐ. Cf. note in vs. 33.

זבד] ܘܙܟܘܪ. Cf. vs. 27. S. reads with 1 Heb. Ms.

ידו]. S. omits.

44. נשאי] ܢܣܒܘ = Ḳ're נָשְׂאוּ.

נשים וישימו] ܐܢܫܐ ܕܐܘܠܕܘ. MT here is corrupt. S. read the same text and tries to express the meaning by "and there were among them men who had begotten sons".

www.ingramcontent.com/pod-product-compliance
Lightning Source LLC
Chambersburg PA
CBHW070100100426
42743CB00012B/2603